THE ROMANTICS

English literature in its historical, cultural and social contexts

Neil King

D0126995

Facts On File, Inc.

The Romantics

Facts On File, Inc.
132 West 31st Street
New York NY 10001

Backgrounds to English Literature
        p. cm.
      Includes bibliographical references and indexes.
      Contents: v. 1. The Renaissance / Patrick Lee-Browne — v. 2. The
    romantics / Neil King — v. 3. The Victorians / Aidan Cruttenden — v. 4.
    The modernist period 1900–1945 / Patrick Lee-Browne — v. 5. Post-war
    literature 1945 to the present / Caroline Merz and Patrick Lee-Browne
      ISBN 0-8160-5125-9 (set : alk. paper) — ISBN 0-8160-5128-3
    (v.2 : alk. paper)
      1. English literature—History and criticism. 2. Literature and history—
    Great Britain. 3. Great Britain—Civilization.

    PR25 .B33 2002
    820.9—dc21   2002071284

Facts On File books are available at special discounts when purchased in bulk
quantities for businesses, associations, institutions, or sales promotions. Please
call our Special Sales Department in New York at
(212) 967-8800 or (800) 322-8755.

You can find Facts On File on the World Wide Web at http://www.factsonfile.com

Printed in Italy by G. Canale and C. S.p.A. - Turin

10 9 8 7 6 5 4 3 2 1

Editor:	Nicola Barber
Consultant:	Dr Essaka Joshua, Department of English, University of Birmingham
Design:	Simon Borrough
Production:	Jenny Mulvanny

Acknowledgements

Cover:	The Bridgeman Art Library
Title page:	The Bridgeman Art Library
p.7:	Copyright the Tate Gallery, London
p.15:	the art archive
p.25:	the art archive
p.29:	The Bridgeman Art Library
p.37:	The National Portrait Gallery, London
p.41:	The Bridgeman Art Library
p.45:	The Bridgeman Art Library
p.53:	The Bridgeman Art Library
p.63:	The Bridgeman Art Library
p.67:	The Bridgeman Art Library
p.69:	The Bridgeman Art Library
p.77:	The Bridgeman Art Library

First published by Evans Brothers Limited, 2A Portman Mansions, Chiltern Street,
London W1U 6NR, United Kingdom

CONTENTS

1. ROMANTICISM

Romanticism is a term applied to a European-wide revolution in literature and other arts covering approximately the period 1780 to 1840. Although German critics used the word *Romantisch* to define certain forms of expression in their own literature, most writers and artists of the time did not apply the term specifically to their work, or speak of living in a 'Romantic era'. As with all periods, eras or ages, the name describing it gradually emerged at a later time when events had settled down and some kind of historical perspective could be seen. The word 'romantic', however, was variously used. By the 17th century it had come to mean 'imaginative', 'fictitious', 'fabulous' or, disapprovingly, 'extravagant'; during the 18th century it came to signify pleasing qualities in a landscape. In his *Dictionary* (1755) Dr Samuel Johnson (1709-84) defined the word as 'Resembling the tales or romances; wild, improbable; false; fanciful; full of wild scenery'; for Samuel Coleridge 'romantic' meant 'imaginative'; and John Keats would have acknowledged 'fanciful' in Johnson's definition as key to the Romantic imagination: 'I am certain of nothing but the holiness of the Heart's affections and the truth of the Imagination'. The Romantic period was destined to be one in which the imaginative gifts of poets, artists and musicians would play a great role in the search for spiritual truth.

— THE KEY PLAYERS —

The six Romantic poets who are most often studied all knew of each other, or at least of each others' work. The first generation comprises William Blake (1757-1827), William Wordsworth (1770-1850) and Samuel Coleridge (1772-1835), the second, younger generation, John Keats (1795-1821), Percy Shelley (1792-1822) and Lord Byron (1788-1824). The main aim of this book is to explore how they, and certain prose writers such as Charles Lamb (1775-1834), Mary Shelley (1797-1851), William Hazlitt (1778-1830), Walter Scott (1771-1832), Thomas Love Peacock (1785-1866) and Thomas De Quincey (1795-1857) fit into the historical, cultural and social contexts of their times.

For the Romantics there was no one – king, politician, general or archbishop – more important than a creative artist. In his Preface to the 1800 edition of the Lyrical Ballads *Wordsworth compares a poet to others as 'a man… endowed with a more lively sensibility, more enthusiasm and tenderness, who has a greater knowledge of human nature, and a more comprehensive soul'. For Shelley, writing in his* Defence of Poetry *(1821), poets were 'the unacknowledged legislators of the world'.*

The origins of Romanticism

The term 'romance' was originally used to describe medieval verse (and occasionally prose) tales, often concerning a chivalric quest and written in one of the romance languages derived from Latin (Catalan, French, Italian, Portuguese, Provençal, Spanish). These tales often involved highly imaginative and heroic adventures in which the honoring of knightly qualities and of women predominated. The quest was later to become a key element for writers such as Byron, whose Childe Harold and Don Juan are essentially questing figures (Byron himself died in the quest for the independence of Greece: see page 28 and Biographical Glossary).

By the 18th century fanciful stories that took place in picturesque or wild settings tended to be called 'romantic'.

From the Renaissance onward the word 'romantic' had often been used negatively to condemn overly imaginative artistic expression that did not accord with Classical purity of form and subject matter. For example, Shakespeare and his English contemporaries frequently broke Aristotle's Classical rules of the Dramatic Unities, which laid down that the action of a play should be located in one place (that is, no multiple locations), that the events of the play should not exceed one day, and that there should be no sub-plots. French and Italian playwrights considered the disregarding of such rules to be an unacceptable freedom of expression that interfered with clarity and precision of thought.

To understand the rise of Romanticism it is necessary to examine the tradition of thinking against which Romanticism was a reaction, looking as far back as the beginning of the Renaissance. That rebirth of learning, which in England is generally dated from the arrival of the Tudors on the throne in 1485, involved among other things a rediscovery of the literature, art, values and general philosophy of Classical Greece and Rome, and an admiration for the clarity of Classical rationality. The intellect and logical thinking were increasingly respected, and this tendency reached its height in the late 17th and early 18th centuries with a movement that became generally known as neo-Classicism ('neo' means 'a new manifestation of'). For example, in literature the taste was for the intelligent wit of writers such as John Dryden (1631-1700), Jonathan Swift (1667-1745), Joseph Addison (1672-1719), Alexander Pope (1688-1744), Henry Fielding (1707-54) and Oliver Goldsmith (c.1730-74); in music, for the mathematical exactitude of the harpsichord; and in architecture for the Classical Ionic and Doric of stately homes such as Blenheim Palace. The first three-quarters of the 18th century is sometimes called the 'Age of Reason' or the 'Enlightenment'.

In simple terms, the Romantics reacted against neo-Classicism, 18th-century rationalism, and the praise of pure intellect; they celebrated instead the importance of feelings and the imagination. Romanticism was also a reaction against a belief, which had gathered force over the 17th and 18th centuries, that science could explain everything concerning human beings. For Blake, mathematics and science were soulless disciplines that chained down people's imaginations and prevented them from expressing themselves with freedom and exuberance. For the Romantics, logic and reason were seen as the servant of Man, not his master.

Another characteristic of the Romantics was a rejection of urban life as the apex of culture. Classical centers of civilization and philosophical thought were cities such as Athens, Rome, Alexandria or, later, Constantinople. During the 18th century there were claims for London and Edinburgh as the centers of British Classicism. Romantic poets, however, increasingly looked toward the countryside for inspiration, finding their most profound experiences in Nature, which was, for them, Man's true setting. The Romantics looked to natural settings, which have the power both to heal and reveal, in order to understand and to fulfill themselves. Examples include George Crabbe (1754-1832), who depicted life in the villages and on the coast of Suffolk, and John Clare (1793-1864), who evoked the agricultural life of his native Northamptonshire. Wordsworth wrote that in Nature he could hear 'the still, sad music of humanity', for:

> 'To her fair works did nature link
> The human soul that through me ran...'
> (from 'Lines Written in Early Spring' 1798)

In his Preface to the second edition of the *Lyrical Ballads* (1800) Wordsworth declared that 'The principal object which I proposed to myself in these Poems was to make the incidents of common life interesting by tracing in them, truly though not ostentatiously, the primary laws of our nature...'. Indeed, it was through rural characters that Wordsworth often chose to trace human nature. His shepherd Michael in the poem of the same name (1800) lives out a dignified country alternative to commercialized and industrialized urban life, emphasized by the rapid corruption of Michael's son in the city. In 'Lines Written a Few Miles Above Tintern Abbey' (1798) Wordsworth wrote of refreshing thoughts of the landscape when 'in lonely rooms, and mid the din/ Of towns and cities' (although in 'Composed upon Westminster Bridge, September 3, 1802' he did admire the beauty of the city soon after dawn, when no fires were alight and everyone was asleep). Shelley wrote, 'Hell is a city much like London'. Blake, above all, saw the evil effects of the Industrial Revolution (see page 46), noting, as he wandered in his imagination through the dirty city streets in 'London' (1794), the mental chains restraining people who

— 'NEW JERUSALEM' —

In The Excursion *(1814) Wordsworth had a vision of an idealized city which, like Blake, he called the 'New Jerusalem':*

> *'The appearance, instantly disclosed,*
> *Was of a mighty city — boldly say*
> *A wilderness of building, sinking far*
> *And self-withdrawn into a wondrous depth*
> *Far sinking into splendour, without end!*
> *Fabric it seemed of diamond and gold,*
> *With alabaster domes, and silver spires,*
> *And blazing terrace upon terrace high*
> *Uplifted: here, serene pavilions bright*
> *In avenues disposed; there, towers begirt*
> *With battlements that on their restless fronts*
> *Bore stars — illumination of all gems!...*
> *Oh 'twas an unimaginable sight!...*
> *That which I saw was the revealed abode*
> *Of spirits in beatitude.'*

———————

William Blake (1757-1827)
Sir Isaac Newton (c.1795)

Blake portrays the famous 18th-century scientist absorbed in precise calculation. The diagram upon which he is working may be useful, but it is a dead thing. Newton is oblivious both to his own natural state of nudity and, more important, to the beauty of the world around him. The image is a condemnation of scientific rationalism, which plans everything and makes everyone 'chartered',—the word Blake used in his poem 'London' to describe the streets, the River Thames and, by implication, all who work in that city. In another picture entitled *The Ancient of Days* (1794), Blake shows a similarly focused and calculating God using compasses as he plans the creation of the world
(see page 60).

were entrapped in a system that enslaved them. Even the fashionable Byron, who wrote somewhat contemptuously in *Don Juan* (1819-24) of the Lake District poets (Wordsworth, Robert Southey [see page 10] and, to a lesser extent, Coleridge) as 'Lakers', increasingly rejected town society.

The main characteristics of Romanticism

In order to understand the contexts of Romanticism it is necessary to identify its main characteristics, insofar as it is possible to be precise about a term that has so many varying definitions and interpretations. The features described in the following paragraphs are not mentioned in any order of importance, but the aspects and contexts that are most important in the work of particular writers will be developed in the chapters that follow. It is appropriate to write of the Romantic movement or writers with a capital 'R' in order to distinguish them from romantic writers who are concerned with sentimental love stories. At its best, Romanticism was a celebration, a life-enhancing hymn of praise to the beautiful things in the world.

Nature

A love of Nature and natural things, which amounted in some to Nature-worship, was key to many Romantics. Their rejection of urban life was not merely a negative move: it was often a positive attitude that within Nature lay an ideal state, free from the artificial aspects of civilization. To be alone in wild, lonely places was for the Romantics to be near to heaven. Having been born in the country town of Ottery St Mary in Devon, Coleridge was sent to Christ's Hospital School in London. In 'Frost at Midnight' (1798), he recalls those school days, when he was:

— SKATING—

During the late 18th and early part of the 19th century there was a succession of very hard winters when rivers and lakes froze over. It is from this period, when Christmas cards first began to be exchanged, that we derive our images of stagecoaches dashing along snow-rutted roads and skaters on the ice. As a young boy Wordsworth took advantage of the freezing conditions and revelled in the feeling of freedom that skating gave:

> *'And in the frosty season, when the sun*
> *Was set, and visible for many a mile,*
> *The cottage windows through the twilight blazed,*
> *I heeded not their summons; clear and loud*
> *The village clock tolled six; I wheeled about*
> *Proud and exulting like an untired horse*
> *That cares not for its home. All shod with steel*
> *We hissed along the polished ice in games*
> *Confederate, imitative of the chase*
> *And woodland pleasures — the resounding horn,*
> *The pack loud bellowing, and the hunted hare.*
> *So through the darkness and the cold we flew,*
> *And not a voice was idle. With the din,*
> *Meanwhile, the precipices rang aloud,*
> *The leafless trees and every icy crag*
> *Tinkled like iron, while the distant hills*
> *Into the tumult sent an alien sound*
> *Of melancholy not unnoticed — while the stars*
> *Eastward were sparkling clear, and in the west*
> *The orange sky of evening died away.'*
> (from The Prelude *1799/1805*)

Wordsworth continued to skate throughout his adult life. Apparently he thought that he was rather good at it, although Coleridge described him as resembling an elephant on ice. Wordsworth's skates are displayed at his home in Dove Cottage, Grasmere.

'... reared
In the great city, pent 'mid cloisters dim
And saw nought lovely but the sky and stars.'

By contrast he goes on to describe his vision of the freedom
that he wishes for the baby (his son) who is peacefully sleeping in a
cradle by his side as he composes the poem:

'But *thou*, my babe! shalt wander like a breeze
By lakes and sandy shores, beneath the crags
Of ancient mountain, and beneath the clouds,
Which image in their bulk both lakes and shores
And mountain crags: so shalt thou see and hear
The lovely shapes and sounds intelligible
Of that eternal language, which thy God
Utters...'

For both Coleridge and Wordsworth, God in Nature was the
'great universal teacher' manifesting himself as the 'spirit and
wisdom of the universe'.

Anti-establishmentism

Closely connected to the Romantics' rejection of the artificial was a
growing opposition to established institutions such as the
monarchy and the Church. In 'The Garden of Love' (1794), Blake
regards the Church as stifling naturalness, with 'Thou shalt not...'
written over the chapel door, and in the Garden of Love where he
used to play freely as a child 'Priests in black gowns were walking
their rounds,/ And binding with briars my joys and desires'. In
Shelley's poem 'The Mask of Anarchy' (written 1819; published
1832), Anarchy, wearing a crown and carrying a scepter, rides a
white horse splashed with blood. As the embodiment of the British
social and political institutions that Shelley hated, he has stamped
on his forehead: 'I AM GOD, AND KING, AND LAW!' (see page 30).
Following on from these attitudes was an embracing of political
and social revolution (see Chapter 2), and above all a sense that
the individual must create his or her own relationship with the
world (see Chapter 3).

The ancient and the exotic

Another frequent Romantic trait was a fascination with other
cultures, different either in time or distance: the old and the
primitive, things medieval or Gothic, Oriental, alien or vanished (the
Romantics would have enjoyed modern science fiction).
Characteristic of this fascination are Coleridge's images of Xanadu
in 'Kubla Khan' (1797) (see page 76) and Keats's world of

medieval romance in 'The Eve of St Agnes' (1820) (see page 80). An important source of inspiration for the Romantics was *Reliques of Ancient English Poetry* (1765, 1794), a selection of ballads by Bishop Thomas Percy (1729-1811). As well as collecting old poems, songs and ballads in English, Percy also translated the same kind of material from Chinese, Hebrew, Old Norse, Scots Gaelic and Spanish.

The supernatural

Following naturally from the Romantic fascination with the old and exotic was an attraction to the supernatural, bizarre or nightmarish. There were elements of the supernatural and bizarre in poetry, such as in the 18th-century Graveyard School of Poetry (see Glossary of Terms), and in the work of Thomas Chatterton (see page 13), Coleridge (*The Rime of the Ancient Mariner* 1798) and Keats ('Isabella' 1820). However, they are most clearly manifested in the Gothic fiction written from the mid-18th century onward (see Chapter 6).

Idealism

Idealism was a keynote for many of the Romantics, perhaps summed up in Blake's words 'Every thing that lives is holy'. Blake had an idealistic vision that this kind of attitude would lead to the creation in Britain of Jerusalem, his word for the perfect, caring government or paradise on Earth. Coleridge's idealism led him to join with the poet Robert Southey (1774-1843) in a plan for setting up the perfect commune in New England. The scheme came to nothing, but not before Coleridge, as part of the plan, had married Southey's sister-in-law – a marriage that turned out to be unhappy (see Biographical Glossary). Political idealism, especially in its hopes for the French Revolution as a new dawn

'EVERY THING THAT LIVES IS HOLY'

Blake's belief that 'Every thing that lives is holy' was implicit in much Romantic writing. For instance, Coleridge believed that all living things were part of a single organism — all life is One Life. The narrator of The Rime of the Ancient Mariner *is forced to learn this lesson, and thereafter is impelled to pass it on. The Ancient Mariner has shot the albatross, had the bird hung round his neck by his ship-mates, and suffered a terrible penance for his wanton vandalism. The curse on him only begins to break when he looks over the side of the ship and marvels at the creatures he sees in the water below:*

'Beyond the shadow of the ship
I watched the water-snakes;
They moved in tracks of shining white,
And when they reared, the elfish light
Fell off in hoary flakes.

Within the shadow of the ship
I watched their rich attire:
Blue, glossy green, and velvet black
They coiled and swam, and every track
Was a flash of golden fire.

Oh happy living things! no tongue
Their beauty might declare:
A spring of love gushed from my heart
And I blessed them unaware!
Sure my kind saint took pity on me,
And I blessed them unaware.

The self-same moment I could pray,
And from my neck so free
The albatross fell off and sank
Like lead into the sea.'

In the same spirit Wordsworth in 'Tintern Abbey' talks of:

'. . . that best portion of a good man's life,
His little, nameless, unremembered acts
Of kindness and of love.'

for mankind, inspired nearly all the early Romantics. These anti-establishment tendencies were continued by Byron, who advanced liberal ideas in the House of Lords, and by Shelley (see pages 28 and 30).

The indulgence of the senses

The exultation of physical sensations and passion for their own sake is another important practice of the Romantics, present in Coleridge but most obvious in the work of the second generation of Keats, Shelley and Byron. In fact, Byron became as famous for his notorious lifestyle as for his poetry, carrying on affairs with such women as the novelist Lady Caroline Lamb (1785-1828).

Carpe diem

Another important Romantic impulse is the notion of *carpe diem* (that is, living for the moment as opposed to spending one's time analyzing the past and planning for the future). Keats once wrote to a friend 'I scarcely remember counting upon any Happiness – I look not for it if it be not in the present hour!'

Romantic pioneers

Jean-Jacques Rousseau (1712-78)

Rousseau was a Genevan-born French writer, philosopher, political theorist and composer who is often regarded as the father of Romanticism. He is a forerunner of much that was later regarded as characteristically Romantic: for example, in his sensitivity, imagination, individualism, closeness to Nature, and rebellion against the established social and political order; and in his belief that reason and intellect are of less importance than are our feelings and emotions, which dictate how our reason operates.

His work exudes a characteristically Romantic energy and passion. He crossed the Alps alone on foot and recorded his impressions in his autobiographical *Confessions* (1782-9). He said: 'I need torrents, rocks, firs, dark woods, mountains, steep roads to climb or descend, abysses beside me to make me afraid.' In this kind of description he points toward the Gothic (see Chapter 6).

— CARPE DIEM (I) —

Shelley's poem 'To a Skylark' (1820) is a fine example of Romantic admiration for a bird that lives entirely for the moment, singing happily, so high in the sky that it can hardly be seen, and unfettered by the intellectual baggage, regrets and longings that cripple human beings:

> *'We look before and after,*
> *And pine for what is not:*
> *Our sincerest laughter*
> *With some pain is fraught:*
> *Our sweetest songs are those that tell of saddest thought.*
>
> *Yet if we could scorn*
> *Hate, and Pride, and Fear;*
> *If we were things born*
> *Not to shed a tear,*
> *I know not how thy joy we ever should come near.'*

Compare this with the box entitled Carpe diem (II) *on page 81.*

He believed that humans must follow 'the promptings of our own nature', and not be bound by social laws of politeness. He considered that the instinctive goodness of people had been corrupted by two things: the acquisition of property ('Property is theft'); and the domination of one person by another. Rousseau noted that people often conspired to perpetuate their own slavery to a system (compare this with Blake's 'mind-forg'd manacles' in 'London'). In his *Discourse* (1754) Rousseau advanced the idea that governments should rule by a contract whereby the monarch obeys the rules of the state and the people obey the monarch. In *The Social Contract* (1762), which begins with the famous sentence 'Man is born free; and everywhere he is in chains', he developed his ideas in republican terms:

> 'In a republic the public voice hardly ever raises to the highest positions men who are not enlightened and capable... while in monarchies those who rise to the top are most often merely petty blunderers, petty swindlers, and petty intriguers, whose petty talents cause them to get into the highest positions at court, but, as soon as they have got there, serve only to make their ineptitude clear to the public. The people is far less often mistaken in its choice than the prince; and a man of real worth among the king's ministers is almost as rare as a fool at the head of a republican government.'

Rousseau believed that education was a vital element in the creation of a better society. In *La Nouvelle Héloïse* (1761) and *Émile, ou l'Education* (1762) he set out the idea that children are born good and innocent, but are corrupted by society; and that they should be allowed to grow instinctively to understand the nature of true freedom and to develop naturally, not being forced into becoming adults before they are ready (compare Rousseau's attitudes with Blake's images of both innocence and corrupted childhood in *Songs of Innocence and of Experience*, 1789 and 1794). In these books Rousseau also advocated fairer treatment of all kinds of workers, and charity toward the poor and unfortunate.

In *Childe Harold's Pilgrimage* (1812-18) Byron paid tribute to Rousseau's idealism, his loving vision of perfect beauty in the world, and the style through which he conveyed his feelings:

> '...he knew
> How to make madness beautiful, and cast
> O'er erring deeds and thoughts a heavenly hue
> Of words, like sunbeams, dazzling as they past
> The eyes, which o'er them shed tears feelingly and fast...'

Shelley wrote to Thomas Love Peacock of 'the divine beauty of Rousseau's imagination'. He venerated the French philosopher's visionary qualities, idealism and hope; and in his unfinished final poem 'The Triumph of Life' (1824), a visionary piece itself, it is the spirit of Rousseau who guides the poet on his journey through life. Rousseau was indeed a guiding ideal for the Romantics, pointing to what was wrong in society but underlining the essential goodness in humanity.

Christopher Smart (1722-71)

A Classical scholar at Cambridge University, Smart was afflicted by mental problems, and for many years his poems were regarded as the work of madness. During the 20th century, however, he gradually came to be recognized as a highly original poet and a forerunner of the Romantics. His unfinished 'Jubilate Agno', based on the verse patterns of Old Testament Hebrew poetry and not published until 1939, is an exuberant celebration of the wonders of Creation. Best known is his loving itemization of the qualities of his cat, a classically Romantic appreciation of a being that rejoices in being itself and living for the day (see *carpe diem* on page 11). The section begins:

> 'For I will consider my cat Jeoffry.
> For he is the servant of the Living God, duly and daily serving him.
> For at the first glance of the glory of God in the East he worships in his way.
> For is this done by wreathing his body seven times round with elegant quickness...'

Thomas Chatterton (1752-70)

Thomas Chatterton's life and early death, as much as his poetry, have an important place in early Romanticism. The posthumous son of a Bristol schoolmaster, Chatterton wrote verses at an early age. He fell in love with things medieval, enthralled by Geoffrey Chaucer and other writers of that period. He started to write poetry in a medieval style, inventing as the author one Thomas Rowley, supposedly a 14th-century Bristol monk and poet. Chatterton constructed a friendship between the fictional Rowley and an actual Bristol merchant called William Canynge, fabricating correspondence between these two, the imaginary and the real, and producing other background documents to support the authenticity of Rowley and his poetry. Chatterton then claimed that he had discovered these manuscripts in an old chest. Why did he not claim them as his own? His motives were mainly to gain credibility for the poetry, a difficult thing for a 16-year-old. In December 1768 he tried to sell the manuscripts to a fashionable

London bookseller, who rejected them. In March 1769 he offered them to the writer Horace Walpole (1717-97), who for a time believed in their authenticity. However, when Walpole discovered the truth, he treated the aspiring poet harshly, at first ignoring Chatterton's pleas for the return of his manuscripts.

Chatterton became very depressed, but was determined to seek his fortune in London, threatening suicide in a successful attempt to cancel an apprenticeship into which he had entered with a local attorney. In April 1770 he set out for London but, despite early optimistic letters home, he struggled against poverty. Despite sometimes having nothing to eat, he sent presents to his mother and sister. When his landlady took pity on the boy and tried to return part of his rent, Chatterton refused the money, pointing to his forehead and saying, 'I have that here which will get me more.'

The circumstances of his death soon after are related in the caption to the illustration opposite. It is no exaggeration to say that Chatterton, whose poems are a subject of fascination as a product of youthful genius but who has rarely been studied in schools, had a considerable impact upon the better-known Romantic poets who followed him. His inventiveness and imagination, and his eye for beauty and color, inspired Coleridge. Wordsworth described him as 'the marvellous Boy, the sleepless Soul that perished in his pride'. Chatterton's early death is a Romantic foreshadowing of the early deaths of all three of the second generation of Romantic poets. Keats dedicated *Endymion* (1818) to him, and wrote a sonnet in his memory:

> 'O Chatterton! how very sad thy fate!
> Dear child of sorrow – son of misery!
> How soon the film of death obscur'd that eye,
> Whence Genius mildly flash'd, and high debate...'
> (from 'Sonnet to Chatterton')

The influence of Chatterton's satires may also be seen in some of Shelley's work. One 19th-century writer paid tribute to him in the terms of a Gothic romance: 'A meteor, shaking from its horrid hair all sorts of evils and disasters, may by-and-by take its place in the clear upper sky, and blend its light with all our day.'

Politics

After the conflict between king and Parliament culminating in the English Civil Wars (1642-51), the execution of Charles I (1649), and the austere Commonwealth period under Oliver Cromwell (1649-60), the monarchy was restored under Charles II (1660). The limitations of royal power and the rights of the citizen were made clearer by the Bill

Henry Wallis (1830-1916)
The Death of Chatterton (1856)

A Victorian critic, John Richmond, described Chatterton's last days as follows: 'In August 1770 the end was drawing near. For a whole week he existed on a single loaf of bread, stale, that it might last longer; his face became wild and haggard, and his eyes burned with an unnatural brightness. Ill and starving, he went one day to the baker and asked for a loaf of bread on credit; it was refused, and on the way back, fixed in his resolve, he procured some arsenic from an apothecary with whom he was acquainted. Next day he did not appear, but faint sounds were heard coming from his apartment. Then silence followed for a day and a night, till his room was broken open, when, lying upon the bed, a few bits of arsenic between his teeth, was found the body of the unfortunate boy.'

of Rights of 1689 (see page 18), two political parties (Tories and Whigs) began to emerge, and by the mid-18th century England was effectively a constitutional monarchy with a system of government run by a Prime Minister and his cabinet, opposed by another political party. However, franchise (the right to vote) was limited to property owners of some substance, and the system was open to abuse – a few bribes from the local landowner could ensure that the 'correct' Member of Parliament (MP) was returned to parliament in an election.

Reform and liberalization were favored by many toward the end of the 18th century, but their minds were changed by the course of the French Revolution after 1789 (see page 26). The increasing barbarities of the Revolution, as seen from the British perspective, led many erstwhile supporters of greater enfranchisement of the people to change their minds: the evidence from France seemed to show that a movement for reform could only end in mob rule. In any event, the outbreak of war between France and Britain in 1793 demanded patriotism. Edmund Burke (1729-97), the spokesman of the aristocratic Tory government of the period, said that the English must treasure and support this 'little platoon' of England, and thoughts of political reform at home were for the moment set aside.

Like the hopes of many others, Coleridge's dreams that the French Revolution would lead to an era of enlightenment and better justice were dashed, and he became disillusioned with politics. In March 1798 he wrote: 'I am of no party. It is true, I think the present ministry weak and perhaps unprincipled men, but I could not with a safe conscience vote for their removal.' By April 1798 fears of a French invasion led him to write in 'Fears in Solitude' (1798) that, with respect to France, 'We have been too long/ Dupes

– WILLIAM GODWIN (1756-1836) –

A novelist, philosopher and biographer, Godwin was the kind of optimistic idealist who had considerable influence over the Romantic poets and other contemporary young minds. A radical, almost anarchic, thinker by the standards of the Age of Reason, and admired by Wordsworth and Coleridge, he became an atheist and believed that humans were rational beings capable of continually improving themselves and thus in no need of institutions or laws. His most important work in this respect was Enquiry concerning Political Justice *(1793) in which he advocated benevolence and community spirit, rejecting selfishness and capitalism. He also agitated for parliamentary reform. He himself was influenced by Rousseau (see page 11) in seeing property as the root of all evil:*

'However great and extensive are the evils that are produced by monarchies and courts, by the imposture of priests and the iniquity of criminal laws, all these are imbecile and impotent, compared with the evils that arise out of the established administration of property.'
(from Enquiry concerning Political Justice*)*

Wordsworth probably met Godwin in February 1795 at a gathering of radical thinkers, and he acknowledged Godwin's influence upon him in sections of The Prelude *written in 1804. However, times changed, Godwin's opinions went out of fashion, and he fell from public view. In 1811 Shelley was surprised to discover that Godwin was still alive. He was much drawn to Godwin's idealism, and began corresponding and meeting with him, as a result of which he fell in love with Godwin's daughter, Mary (later the author of* Frankenstein *[1818]: see page 78), and eloped with her. Godwin's liberalism did not extend to condoning this behavior. By the 1820s Godwin's earlier radicalism had dimmed. He was married briefly to the early feminist writer Mary Wollstonecraft (1759-97), author of* A Vindication of the Rights of Woman *(1792), who died soon after giving birth to their daughter.*

_____

of a deep delusion...'. He went on to bemoan the fact that, as a radical, he was branded an enemy of Britain by those in authority, affirming his patriotism in ringing terms:

'But native Britain! Oh my mother isle!
How shouldst thou prove aught else but dear and holy
To me, who from thy lakes and mountain-hills,
Thy clouds, the quiet dales, thy rocks, and seas,
Have drunk in all my intellectual life.
All sweet sensations, all ennobling thoughts,
All adoration of the God in nature,
Whatever makes this mortal spirit feel
The joy and greatness of its future being?
There lives nor form nor feeling in my soul
Unborrowed from my country! Oh divine
And beauteous island, thou hast been my sole
And most magnificent temple, in the which
I walk with awe, and sing my stately songs,
Loving the God that made me!'

A few years later, Blake's love of England and its 'mountains green', 'pleasant pastures' and 'clouded hills' did not dull his vision of a country where 'Jerusalem', that state of justice, equality and freedom for all, might be established, and where ghastly factories, those 'dark Satanic mills', might be abolished:

'I will not cease from mental fight
Nor shall my sword sleep in my hand,
Till we have built Jerusalem
In England's green and pleasant land.'
(from 'Milton: A Poem in Two Books, To Justify the Ways of God to Men' 1803-8)

After the Napoleonic Wars finally came to an end in 1815 with the Battle of Waterloo, power in England passed into the hands of a right-wing Tory government which was hated and despised by most Romantics. Shelley's attacks were forthright, and his view of the state of the nation in 1819 was summed up in the following sonnet ('Sonnet: England in 1819'; see also on pages 30-1 the extracts from 'The Mask of Anarchy', written in the same year). The 'Phantom' at the end is almost certainly political revolution:

'An old, mad, blind, despised, and dying king, –
Princes, the dregs of their dull race, who flow
Through public scorn, – mud from a muddy spring, –
Rulers who neither see, nor feel, nor know,

But leech-like to their fainting country cling
Till they drop, blind in blood, without a blow, –
A people starved and stabbed in the untilled field, –
An army, which liberticide and prey
Makes as a two-edged sword to all who wield, –
Golden and sanguine laws which tempt and slay
Religion Christless, Godless – a book sealed;
A Senate – Time's worst statute unrepealed, –
Are graves, from which a glorious Phantom may
Burst, to illuminate our tempestuous day.'

It was another 13 years before the country started to reform Parliament as a step on the way toward greater democracy (see page 31).

The Empire

In 1688 both political parties, the Whigs and the Tories, combined to overthrow the Catholic king, James II. They invited the Protestant Dutch king, William of Orange, to rule jointly with his wife Mary, James's Protestant daughter. William accepted both the throne and a Bill of Rights (1689). This Bill recognized the authority of Parliament as representative of the will of the people, and that British monarchs no longer ruled by divine right. The so-called 'Glorious Revolution' (because it happened without bloodshed) led to greater stability in Britain and served as a basis for expansion of trade and territory abroad. The beginning of the creation of the British Empire reflected an increasing confidence among the British people. The ambitions of Louis XIV of France had been contained, notably by the victories of the Duke of Marlborough in the early 18th century. In the middle of the century the French challenge to British power in India was overcome by Robert Clive (1725-74), and in Canada by James Wolfe (1727-59). Further afield, Captain James Cook (1728-79) explored the South Pacific and extended Britannia's grasp to Australia and the Polynesian Islands. However, the American Revolution and subsequent loss of the American colonies in the latter part of the century was very damaging to this emergent national pride (see page 21).

—THE COSMOPOLITAN—

Most of the Romantic poets were more cosmopolitan in their outlook than writers of previous ages. For example, Wordsworth and Coleridge travelled widely on the Continent, especially in France, and Wordsworth and his sister Dorothy spent time during the bitterly cold winter of 1798 in Goslar in the Hartz Mountains of Germany, learning German in order to seek work as translators. Byron and Shelley hated the hypocrisy and oppression that they saw in English society after the end of the Napoleonic Wars, finding inspiration through their travels in Switzerland, Italy and Byron's beloved Greece. They finally settled in Italy, Shelley on the northwest Ligurian coast and Byron in Venice, whose romantic decay he found alluring. Much of Byron's wanderings over Europe became material for Childe Harold's Pilgrimage *and* Don Juan.

The Industrial Revolution

Advances in science and developments in machinery during the 18th century foreshadowed the Industrial Revolution which rapidly gathered speed during the Romantic period. In 1779, Abraham Darby (1750-91) completed the world's first iron bridge, built across the River Severn in Shropshire. Another key figure was Thomas Telford (1757-1834), a Scottish engineer, who constructed many canals, roads and bridges, and was a friend of the poet Robert Southey. Canals may appear to be a relatively slow means of transport by today's standards, but they greatly increased the speed with which raw materials and manufactured goods could be transported from one part of the country to another. A fuller discussion of the Industrial Revolution and its impact appears in Chapter 4.

The reading public

Before the 18th century, those who could read were mainly gentry, clergymen, and educated professional people, and most of their leisure reading was poetry. The early 18th century saw a large rise in the number of people, mainly middle-class ladies, who had the time to read, and it was just at this time that the novel emerged to cater for what was soon to become a mass taste. Daniel Defoe (1660-1731) is often regarded as the first novelist with *Robinson Crusoe* (1719) and *Moll Flanders* (1722), and as the century wore on the works of Fielding, Samuel Richardson (1689-1761), Tobias Smollett (1721-71), Laurence Sterne (1713-68) and others became fashionable reading material. By the end of the century the craze was for the Gothic novel (see Chapter 6). The domestic novels of Jane Austen (1775-1817) enjoyed limited popularity at the time (see page 75). They may, however, have influenced Scott, who admired Austen and favorably reviewed *Emma* (1816): when he moved from writing poetry to novels he tended to create characters who, within a Romantic setting with Romantic ideas, have their idealism tested (and sometimes found inadequate) in the face of hard reality.

Poetry still held its place, but it increasingly reserved for itself the status of an elevated form of writing that used a specialized language known as 'poetic diction' (see Glossary of Terms). It is in this context that Wordsworth attempted to introduce to the poetry-reading public the idea that poems could be written in the language of ordinary people (and also be about ordinary people). In the Preface to the first (1798) edition of the *Lyrical Ballads* he wrote that the poems in the collection 'were written chiefly with a view to ascertain how far the language of conversation in the middle and lower classes of society is adapted to the purposes of poetic pleasure. Readers accustomed to the gaudiness and inane phraseology of many modern writers, if they persist in reading this book to its conclusion, will perhaps frequently have to struggle with feelings of strangeness and awkwardness.'

Of all the writers of the Romantic period, only Byron and Scott, the popularizer of the historical novel, sold enough of their work to achieve commercial success. Buying books could be a costly business: Scott's *Waverley* (1814) and Austen's *Emma* cost a guinea apiece (£1.05) – by present-day standards a phenomenal price for a book – although they were beautifully produced and leather-bound. There were no cheap paperback editions (an increasing number of inexpensive board editions started to appear in the late 1840s). Yet the rise of 'circulating libraries', from which books could be borrowed, allowed more and more people ready access to books. In *The Rivals* (1775) by the Irish playwright Richard Brinley Sheridan (1751-1816), Sir Anthony Absolute declares: 'A circulating library in a town is an ever-green tree of diabolical knowledge!'.

2. THE AGE OF REVOLUTION

The American Revolution

In 1763, British power in North America reached its height. Along with the 13 colonies, settled by British colonizers since the 16th century, Britain now controlled vast territories as far east as the Mississippi River. These territories were handed over by France after its defeat in the Seven Years' War. Yet, within only 12 years, British troops were once more fighting in North America, this time against the American colonists themselves. One of the main reasons behind the American Revolutionary War was dissatisfaction over taxation. In an attempt to increase revenue from its American colonies, the British Parliament introduced several unpopular taxes, including the Sugar Act (1764) and the Stamp Act (1765). Without their own Members of Parliament in Britain, the colonists had no legitimate way of arguing their case against these acts. Another reason for resentment was that Britain wished to maintain good relations with the Native American population; as a result the government issued a Proclamation (1763) to prevent the colonists from expanding their settlements east of the Appalachian Mountains.

In 1774, representatives of each of the 13 colonies met at the First Continental Congress to discuss what action to take against the British government. In 1775 at Lexington, Massachusetts, fighting broke out between American colonists and British soldiers, and the first shots of the American Revolution were fired. An American army was formed under the leadership of George Washington (1732-99), and on 4 July 1776 the Americans declared their independence from Britain. The fighting dragged on for five years, and often the British seemed to be winning, despite help for the colonists from France. The Americans finally achieved victory in 1781, and two years later Britain recognized America as an independent country.

The American Revolution was the first war of colonial liberation, and as such inevitably drew the attention of liberals in Britain. Europeans saw in the American

— A PERSPECTIVE ON THE —
AMERICAN REVOLUTION

Even a visionary poet such as Blake, who often seemed to be on a different plane from contemporary politics, was responsive to events such as the American Revolution. For example, in the following extract we see that Blake not only knows about leading American political figures such as George Washington and Benjamin Franklin (1706-90), but also of American military generals such as Horatio Gates (1728-1806) and Nathanael Greene (1742-86). Albion is the old mythical name for Britain, and thus the Prince of Albion is the British state:

> *'The Guardian Prince of Albion burns in his*
> *   nightly tent,*
> *Sullen fires across the Atlantic glow to America's*
> *   shore,*
> *Piercing the souls of warlike men, who rise in*
> *   silent night,*
> *Washington, Franklin, Paine and Warren, Gates,*
> *   Hancock and Greene*
> *Meet on the coast glowing with blood from*
> *   Albion's fiery Prince.'*

(from America, A Prophecy 1793)

_____

21

example a symbol of hope for those who suffered under oppressive absolute monarchies. Yet not all Americans supported the Revolutionary War or wished to break away from Britain. The outcome was largely determined by the willpower of the American ruling elite, led by George Washington, to forge a new nation. The war was no popular uprising of the people: most of those at the forefront of the rebellion were landowners of some wealth. Nevertheless, one of the guiding principles of the Founding Fathers of the United States Constitution was that every individual, no matter how humble her or his background, had equal rights. The American Revolution did not give rise to a movement for popular socialism as did the 18th- and 19th-century revolutions in Europe: indeed, the background of American protest, starting with the original immigrants, was one of non-conformism, of being free to determine one's own way of life and thinking. (See Chapter 3 for more on this aspect of individualism and American Transcendentalism.)

The situation in Europe

The major event early in the Romantic era, and arguably the most important one, was the social and political upheaval that began in 1789, known as the French Revolution. During the 18th century certain European monarchs, who became known as 'enlightened despots', saw that political, administrative, economic, legal and social reforms were needed in their countries. Many early 18th-century French thinkers admired moves in England to curb royal power (see page 18). Toward the end of the century, rulers such as Catherine the Great (1729-96) in Russia, Frederick the Great (1712-86) in Prussia and Joseph II (1765-90) of Austria initiated programs of reform, but such imaginative moves were

—**THOMAS PAINE (1737-1809)**—

Thomas Paine was a political writer whose democratic and free-thinking philosophies inspired some of the political and social aspects of Romanticism. The son of an East Anglian artisan, in 1774 he was fired from his job as a customs officer for trying to get higher pay for himself and his fellow workers. In 1776 he went to America and wrote a series of pamphlets supporting, amongst other things, American independence from Britain and the emancipation of women, and opposing slavery. He returned to Britain in 1791 and wrote his most important book, The Rights of Man *(published in two parts, 1791 and 1792), in reply to* Reflections on the Revolution in France *(1790) by Edmund Burke. In the face of the events in France, Burke had argued that all men were not naturally equal and that traditional and long-established social and political institutions should be upheld. Paine countered that each generation should make its own decisions on how to rule and conduct itself, free from the constraining traditions of previous ages; in this he was in accord with the Romantic notion that each individual must find her or his own pathway through the world, unhampered by social, political or religious presuppositions:*

'When all the governments of Europe shall be established on the representative system, nations will become acquainted, and the animosities and prejudices fomented by the intrigues and artifices of courts will cease. The oppressed soldier will become a free man, and the tortured sailor, no longer dragged through the streets like a felon, will pursue his mercantile voyage in safety.'
(from The Rights of Man)

Paine's plea for the freedom of democracy was seen as both dangerous and destabilizing by the British government, and he was forced to flee to France to escape arrest. It is apt that Blake, whose beliefs — especially concerning the tyranny of established religion — were similar to Paine's, warned Paine of his impending arrest. Paine's views made him welcome in revolutionary France, but his opposition to the execution of Louis XVI landed him in prison and in danger of the guillotine himself. He returned to America in 1802.

———————

not universally welcomed. Local resentment was caused by the strong, centralizing hand used to enforce reforms. Many landowners and others who had held power under the old system opposed anything that would reduce their influence. This was especially so in the Austrian Empire, where Joseph II incensed the aristocracy, landowners and the Church by attempting to reduce the tax exemptions of the rich, abolish serfdom, and cut down the power of the Catholic Church.

In Britain the anti-Catholic Gordon riots of 1780 were the only times when a lower-class mob seemed to threaten the establishment. The Gordon riots (named after Lord George Gordon, leader of the Protestant Association) lasted for nearly a week, and terrorized much of London. Nonetheless, troops who had gone to America and fought for the revolutionary cause were back in Europe after 1783, and on hand as revolutionary ferment increased in the late 1790s. It has been said that revolution could have broken out in any of a number of European states in the late 18th century: but it was in France, the most culturally advanced, centralized, powerful and populous of European countries, that an authoritarian monarchy and a lack of any move toward meaningful representative government made the conditions ideal for revolution.

The French Revolution

Between the 16th and 18th centuries the monarchy in France gained enormous power, supported by the aristocracy. Those in authority were unwilling to compromise their power through any measure of reform, and thus became increasingly unpopular with the ordinary people. In May 1789, King Louis XVI was almost bankrupt; for the first time since 1614, the king was forced to call a parliament (known as the Estates General) in order to raise taxes. The Estates General refused the king's demands and formed a new National Assembly with the aim of establishing a new constitution in France. The king and his supporters reacted by calling in the army, which had the effect of stirring up popular support for the revolutionaries. In July 1789 a mob in Paris stormed the Bastille prison, symbol of royal power and oppression, and more uprisings followed across the country. On 4 August 1789, the National Assembly summed up the spirit of the Revolution in the 'Declaration of the Rights of Man and the Citizen'. This declaration abolished the old methods of taxation, and greatly reduced the power of the king and the aristocracy. It also established that all citizens had the same basic rights. Between 1789 and 1792 the nobility was abolished, the king was imprisoned, and the right to vote was extended to all adult males. In 1792, the new National Convention opened and declared France a Republic, under the slogan 'Liberty, Equality, Fraternity'.

In January 1793, Louis XVI was executed on a charge of treason. His beheading on the guillotine marked the beginning of a year in which the Revolution became increasingly violent. The two opposing factions in the Convention, the Jacobins and the Girondins, fought bitterly for power, and in June 1793 the Jacobins won the struggle. Many leading Girondins were arrested and summarily killed. Under the leadership of Maximilien Robespierre (1758-94) and others, the Jacobins presided over a 'Reign of Terror' in which anyone who disagreed with their policies was hunted down and executed. However, in July 1794, Robespierre was himself put to death on the guillotine, bringing the Reign of Terror to a close. A new government was formed, called the Directory, but it did away with many of the revolutionary reforms, including universal male suffrage.

It was around this time that a young man from a poor Corsican family began to rise to power. From 1792, France had been at war with many countries in Europe, including Britain, and under the leadership of Napoleon Bonaparte (1769-1821), the French army won some notable campaigns. In 1799, the military hero also became the First Consul of France, when Napoleon seized control of the government. His actions brought the French Revolution to an end.

—The Cult of Nature— and the Republican Calendar

During the French Revolution there grew up a Cult of Nature which replaced established religion. One by-product of this was the replacing of the traditional calendar with a new, Republican version. The first year began on 1 September 1792, each of the 12 months was divided into three décades of ten days each, and all the months were poetically renamed after aspects of Nature's seasons. For example, the first month was Vendémaire, after the vendage (grape harvest); the second Brumaire, after the brume (mists) of autumn; the third, Frimaire (frost); the eighth Floréal, after the flowers of spring; the twelfth Fructidor, after the fruits of summer. The last day of each décade was a rest day, and the five or six days left over at the end of the year were given over as festivals to celebrate Genius, Labor, Opinion, Rewards and Virtue. In theory, the calendar should have worked well, but in practice it made for chaotic communications with other countries. Napoleon abandoned it in 1806 and returned to the traditional calendar.

Romantic reactions to revolution – the first generation

The first generation of Romantic poets, Blake, Coleridge and Wordsworth, were passionately enthusiastic about revolution and possible future developments toward democracy. The young Coleridge advocated republicanism in his writings and lectures. Wordsworth spoke in *The Prelude* of:

'France standing on the top of golden hours,
And human nature seeming born again.'

And, even more excitedly, he wrote: 'Bliss was it in that dawn to be alive/ But to be young was very heaven.'

Eugène Delacroix (1798-1863)
Liberty Leading the People **(1830)**
Delacroix's portrayal of the bare-breasted young woman leading
the revolutionaries forward is a classic Romantic image of the
drive toward freedom and democracy for ordinary people.

However, it is important for the modern reader to appreciate that 'democracy' was a dirty word for the British political and social establishment of the time, and that the idea of ordinary people having the right to vote in elections was viewed by many people with horror. Many of the views of Wordsworth and Coleridge struck their contemporaries as politically dangerous.

The initial fervor of Wordsworth and others for the Revolution in France was sustained until 1792, but after the execution of King Louis XVI, doubts grew. During 1793, the English Romantic idealists watched with increasing anxiety the struggles of 1793 and the Reign of Terror that followed. Despite all this, English Romantics maintained their vision that in France lay the best possibility for a fairer political and social order.

Britain's declaration of war on France in 1793 (in response to the French declaration on Britain, the Netherlands and Spain), angered Coleridge and Wordsworth; the latter even applauded French victories, declaring himself a Republican and accepting that sometimes violence was necessary during the establishment of a new order. Eventually Wordsworth's opinion began to turn, especially after Robespierre brought in a law (1794) by which suspects could be condemned without a proper trial. Denunciations were frequent and informers flourished in the fearful atmosphere in France. In *The Prelude*, Wordsworth wrote:

> 'Tyrants, strong before
> In devilish pleas, were ten times stronger now;
> And thus beset with foes on every side
> The goaded land waxed mad; the crimes of few
> Spread into madness of the many; blasts
> From hell came sanctified like airs from heaven.'

Wordsworth went on to rejoice at the fall of Robespierre as an opportunity for a new beginning for the Revolution, but his optimism was short-lived. He became increasingly disillusioned with events in France, lamenting 'what man has made of man'.

For Coleridge, a key event was the French invasion in 1798 of Switzerland, often regarded as a symbol of freedom. On 16 April 1798 he published in *The Morning Post* a poem entitled 'France: an Ode' in which he repented his enthusiasm of the early 1790s for Switzerland's 'cruel foes'. In September 1799 he wrote to Wordsworth of 'those who, in consequence of the complete failure of the French Revolution, have thrown up all hopes of the amelioration of mankind'. However, during the late 1790s the attitude of the English Romantics was still ambivalent. By 1802 Wordsworth was asking in his ode 'Intimations of Immortality' (written 1802; published 1807): 'Whither is fled the visionary gleam? Where is it now, the glory and the dream?' The issue became much clearer with the rise of Napoleon: he declared himself Emperor in 1804, marking himself as a tyrant whom the Romantics could oppose unequivocally. Yet the Romantics could draw little comfort from the leadership of their own country, where strong liberal politicians were non-existent and powerful generals such as Arthur Wellesley, Duke of Wellington (1769-1852) dominated affairs. The mood of the time among Romantics is summed up by the essayist William Hazlitt:

> 'For my part, I set out in life with the French Revolution, and that event had considerable influence on my early feelings, as on those of others... It was the dawn of a new era, a new impulse had been given to men's minds, and the sun of Liberty rose upon the sun of Life in the same day... Little did I dream, while my first hopes and wishes went hand in hand with those of the human race, that long before my eyes should close, that dawn would be overcast, and set once more in the night of despotism – "total eclipse!"'
> (from *On the Feeling of Immortality in Youth*)

Yet however much the early Romantics lost their zest for political revolution as time went on, they maintained their revolutionary vision of changing the world for the better.

After the French and American revolutions, the Age of Revolution was far from over. There may have been a pause during the Napoleonic Wars, which compelled the nations of Europe to think more about their national identity than about wider social issues, but as soon as those wars concluded in 1815, the spirits of Romanticism, liberalism and socialism emerged or re-emerged, and there was a series of domestic disturbances across Europe leading up to 1848, the 'Year of Revolutions'. Those who manned the barricades in Paris during the various revolutions of these years were not the lowest laboring classes, but predominantly skilled workers and craftworkers – the kind of people with whom Blake would have identified. The novelist Victor Hugo (1802-85), a leading member of the French Romantic movement, wrote of the activities of such people at the barricades in *Les Misèrables* (1862).

Blake had a vision, in common with a hope once held by Milton, that paradise on Earth ('Jerusalem') might be achieved through politics; he saw 'a world in a grain of sand', and envisaged that the world might one day see the beauty of the humble as clearly as he did. When Wordsworth fixed his attention on the humble Leech Gatherer, assorted beggars and broken old soldiers, he was doing a similar thing. Explicitly or implicitly, both Blake and Wordsworth were yearning for democracy.

Romantic reactions to revolution – the second generation

The second generation of Romantic poets, Byron, Keats and Shelley, lived their creative years under repressive Tory governments who were terrified that any political reforms might trigger a revolution. The outlet for Byron's revolutionary zeal was the fight for Greek independence. Byron had always been attracted to this cause (see *Childe Harold's Pilgrimage*): the idea that the cradle of democracy was subjugated to a foreign power was anathema to him, and in 1822, when the Greeks rose up in revolt against their Turkish overlords, he felt that the moment had come for him to express his ideals in action. He joined the Greek partisans, but the adventure cost him his life when, before he saw any action, he died of fever at Missolonghi.

Both Keats and Shelley expressed anti-monarchist views in their poetry, but it was Shelley who was most deeply influenced by the events of the French Revolution and who continued to write overtly political poetry. Inspired by the example of the events in France, despite the eventual failure of the Revolution, Shelley set out his ideal of a peaceful revolution in a long poem 'The Revolt of Islam' (1817). In his 'lyrical drama', *Prometheus Unbound* (1820), he described an ideal state in which monarchy no longer exists and all people are equal:

> 'And behold, thrones were kingless, and men walked
> One with the other even as spirits do,
> None fawned, none trampled...
> The loathsome mask has fallen, the man remains
> Sceptreless, free, uncircumscribed, but man
> Equal, unclassed, tribeless, and nationless
> Exempt from awe, worship, degree, the king
> Over himself...'

Against the background of revolution, it is unsurprising that the late Romantic period saw the beginnings of socialism as we understand the word. In the face of the grim industrialization opposed by Blake and others, and despite the liberal Romantic belief in the freedom of the individual to pursue and protect her or his own interests, there developed ideas of how society might be organized along lines of greater equality and fairness, including equal democratic political rights for all. It may be that the passing of the Reform Act in 1832 (see page 31) saved England from the series of revolutions that swept Europe between 1830 and 1848.

James Gillray (1757-1815)
***'The Blood of the Murdered crying for Vengeance'* (1793)**

The grotesque style of this cartoon gives an impression of the revulsion felt in Britain at the execution of the French king, Louis XVI, on 21 January 1793. Like many people in Britain, Gillray was initially sympathetic to the ideals of the Revolution, even marking its first anniversary by engraving a print celebrating the taking of the Bastille. However, this engraving shows the blood of the executed king literally crying out for vengeance: 'revenge the blood of a Monarch most undeservedly butchered, and rescue the Kingdom of France…'

The Peterloo Massacre

The Reform Act of 1832 was the culmination of many years of agitation for parliamentary reform. One of the main issues at stake was the lack of representation in Parliament for towns and cities that had grown rapidly as a result of the Industrial Revolution (see page 46). While some small towns which had once been important commercial centers had one or two Members of Parliament (MPs), large towns and cities such as Manchester and Birmingham had no MPs at all. In 1819, reformers decided to focus attention on the need for change by calling mass meetings in some of these towns and cities. Accordingly, on 16 August 1819, a crowd of 60,000 men, women and children, mainly working-class handloom weavers, assembled at St Peter's Field, Manchester, to hear speakers on various matters including parliamentary reform and the repeal of the Corn Laws (taxes which pushed up the price of bread and caused great hardship, especially among the urban poor). The militia was sent to break up the meeting, charged the crowd, and caused at least 11 deaths and hundreds of injuries. The name Peterloo was given to the scene of the killings as an ironic comment on a Tory government that claimed credit for the defeat and death of the enemies of Britain at Waterloo four years before, yet was now slaughtering its own people at a peaceful demonstration. The main speaker at the meeting, Henry Hunt, was tried and acquitted of conspiracy and sedition, a verdict heralded as a triumph for liberal justice. He was greeted in London by mass popular acclaim on 18 September 1819.

When Shelley, by then living in permanent, self-imposed exile in Italy, heard of the Peterloo Massacre he wrote 'The Masque of Anarchy', a vicious satire on the Tory government, paradoxically equating their laws and rule with anarchy (that is, lawlessness and lack of rule). For example, he personified Lord Castlereagh, the Home Secretary, as 'Murder', and Eldon, the Lord Chancellor, as 'Fraud':

'I met Murder on the way –
He had a mask like Castlereagh
Very smooth he looked, yet grim;
Seven blood-hounds followed him:

All were fat; and well they might
Be in admirable plight,
For one by one, and two by two,
He tossed them human hearts to chew
Which from his wide cloak he drew.

Next came Fraud, and he had on,
Like Eldon, an ermined gown;
His big tears, for he wept well,
Turned to mill-stones as they fell.

And the little children, who
Round his feet played to and fro,
Thinking every tear a gem,
Had their brains knocked out by them.'

The poem continues in this manner for 61 stanzas, ending with an exhortation to the people of England to rise up in revolt against their masters:

'Rise like Lions after slumber
In unvanquishable number –
Shake your chains to earth like dew
Which in sleep had fallen on you –
Ye are many – they are few.'

Shelley's freedom of speech was not appreciated in the England of the time, and nobody dared to publish the poem. With Shelley beyond reach across the sea in Italy, any publisher would have risked the full anger of the Establishment. It is ironic that 'The Mask of Anarchy' was eventually printed in 1832, the year of parliamentary reform.

The 1832 Reform Act

By the 1830s, the wiser of Britain's leaders saw that if reform did not come from within Parliament it would come through a bloody revolution. The arch-Tory Duke of Wellington (1769-1852) held out against change for as long as possible, but in November 1830 his Tory government was defeated and the more forward-looking Whigs took power under the prime ministership of Lord Charles Grey (1764-1845). 'There is no doubt,' commented the Whig MP Lord John Russell (1792-1878) as he introduced the First Reform Bill to Parliament, 'that the House of Commons as it now exists does not represent the people of England. A stranger who was told that this country once in every seven years elects representatives from its population, would be very much astonished if he were to see large and opulent towns, full of enterprise and

— 'OZYMANDIAS' —

Shelley's opinions about tyrannical power were probably expressed most succinctly in his sonnet, written in 1817 and published in the following year, 'Ozymandias':

'I met a traveller from an antique land
Who said: Two vast and trunkless legs of stone
Stand in the desert… Near them, on the sand,
Half sunk, a shattered visage lies, whose frown,
And wrinkled lip, and sneer of cold command,
Tell that its sculptor well those passions read
Which yet survive, stamped on these lifeless things,
The hand that mocked them, and the heart that fed;
And on the pedestal these words appear:
"My name is Ozymandias, king of kings:
Look on my works, ye Mighty, and despair!"
Nothing besides remains. Round the decay
Of that colossal wreck, boundless and bare
The lone and level sands stretch far away.'

industry and intelligence... and were then told that these towns sent no representatives to Parliament... The House will show the world that it is determined no longer to be an assembly of the representatives of small classes and particular interests, but that it is resolved to form a body of men who represent the people, who spring from the people, who have sympathies with the people.'

Lord Russell might have been speaking with the youthful Wordsworth's attitude toward poetry or Shelley's revolutionary fervor in mind. The First Reform Bill of April 1831 was narrowly defeated, but in September the Second Reform Bill was passed by 106 votes. When the House of Lords, protecting the self-interest of many of its members, threw it out, there was great anger. There were riots in Derby and Bristol, and throughout the country associations and unions were set up to agitate for reform. When the Third Reform Bill was passed by the Commons by an even greater majority and then had most of its important provisions cut down by the Lords, the country appeared to be on the brink of civil war. In this extremity, Grey threatened that the House of Lords should be flooded by newly created peers in order to force through the Reform Bill. As a result, Wellington and many anti-reform peers absented themselves on 4 June 1832, leaving those in the House of Lords to pass the Bill, which thus at last became law. More than one hundred 'pocket' and 'rotten' boroughs (see Glossary of Terms) were abolished, and many town and country areas were given MPs for the first time. However, it was another 50 years before the kind of democratic revolution envisaged by the Romantics in which votes were given to men regardless of wealth and class; and yet another 50 years before all had the vote regardless of gender.

— THE CHARTISTS—

The Chartists were members of a political movement of the 1830s and 1840s, mainly radical intellectuals and industrial workers who aspired to bring about many of the liberal political reforms which were among the ideals of the Romantics. They criticized the Reform Act of 1832 for not extending the vote to the working man, and in 1838 published a 'People's Charter' which demanded votes for all men, abolition of property qualifications and payment for MPs, voting by secret ballot, equal representation in each electoral district, and annual elections for parliament. With the exception of the latter, all the Chartists' aims were eventually realized.

3. INDIVIDUALISM

Romantic poetry created a shift in emphasis in English literature: whereas poetry of the Augustan (see Glossary of Terms) and neo-Classical periods focused on collective morality and public concerns, from the Romantic period onward poetry became more focused on personal experience. For example, in 1733 Alexander Pope published a lengthy poem entitled *Essay on Man*, exploring among other things mankind's collective philosophical place within the universe. By contrast, toward the end of the same century Wordsworth began to write *The Prelude*, a long poem focused upon his own particular experience and the growth of his individual mind. Wordsworth continued to work on this poem until his death more than 50 years later.

Rousseau, one of the earliest Romantic thinkers (see page 11), was in many respects an individualist, seeking solitude for his thoughts on long journeys into wild, remote landscapes. Wordsworth, likewise, spoke of 'the bliss of solitude' and seemed endlessly to have rejoiced in his own company. In their poems the Romantics often created characters, or *personae* (see Glossary of Terms), in which they saw themselves as isolated figures, rejoicing in solitude but not necessarily lonely. For example, Coleridge wrote of his home at Nether Stowey, under the shadow of the Quantock Hills in Somerset:

'The inmates of my cottage, all at rest,
Have left me to that solitude, which suits
Abstruser musings: save that at my side
My cradled infant slumbers peacefully.
'Tis calm indeed! So calm, that it disturbs
And vexes meditation with its strange
And extreme stillness.'
(from 'Frost at Midnight')

However, despite celebrating 'that solitude, which suits/ Abstruser musings…' Coleridge was at heart a gregarious man, and needed to return frequently to the society of people.

The Romantic emphasis on individual perception led to a change regarding the function of the poet. Romantics began to see the business of the poet not as 'holding the mirror up to Nature', but as shaping Nature through their individual and unique perceptions of it. The example may be considered of a tree in the middle of an open field. Different viewers may see it from different angles, and thus have different 'truths' to impart about its shape, color and lighting. Yet it is the same tree. The varying perceptions of the tree add to our knowledge of it; at the same time our examination of each individual perception of the tree adds to our knowledge of humanity and the ways there are for an individual to see things. Wordsworth wrote to Coleridge about *The Prelude* that it was 'unprecedented in literary history that a man should talk so much about himself', and the remarkable thing is that it was true: such self-examination had not been undertaken before the Romantics. Likewise, in previous times the general wisdom for artists was that they became great by imitating their illustrious forebears (see Chapter 5); yet Wordsworth spoke for the Romantic generation when he said: 'Never forget that every great and original writer must himself create the taste by which he is to be relished.'

Romantics and religion

The Romantic poets were not conformists to the institutions of the state or the Church; instead they assumed their own moral authority, following their own pathways in the world. Doubt as regards faith and God had increased during the 'Age of Reason' (see page 5). In general, the Romantics believed that there must be a God who inspired the imaginative and spiritual in humans. In 'Frost at Midnight' Coleridge saw God in Nature as the 'Great universal teacher'; and the young Wordsworth wrote that:

> 'There is an active principle alive
> In all things – in all natures...
> ... – yet is reverenced least
> And least respected in the human mind,
> Its most apparent home.'
> (from 'There is an active principle' 1798)

In 'Joan of Arc' (1796), Southey put into Joan's mouth his own feelings when she speaks of 'Gods priest-created', and of:

> '...the bounds
> Subtle and narrow which confine the path
> Of orthodox belief... 'Twas nature taught my early youth
> Religion; nature bade me see the God
> Confessed in that lives, and moves, and is.'

In a sonnet addressed to Shelley, Leigh Hunt wrote that men, notwithstanding all the beauty of the world around them, have to create a God: '...a phantom, swelled into grim size/ Out of their own passions and bigotries...' (from 'To Percy Shelley, on the degrading Notions of Deity' 1818).

In religious matters the Romantic tendency was toward non-conformism, rejecting established religion and orthodox Christianity in search of other kinds of spiritualism tailored by each individual.

The Romantics wanted no Church and priesthood between themselves and their God. However, it is important to distinguish this approach from atheism, which the Romantics (with the exception of Shelley) abhorred. Blake may have seen God as an evil creator: nevertheless God did exist for Blake – an individual God for an individual visionary.

Exterior and interior landscapes

Wordsworth's reaction to the increasing commercialization and industrialization of his time was to draw inspiration from his perception of an exterior landscape, analyzing his personal response to it. He believed that this gave him insight into 'the still sad music of humanity'. Coleridge, too, experienced the exterior landscape with a keen intensity. In 1797 he wrote 'This Lime-Tree Bower my Prison', which was addressed to Charles Lamb. While some friends were staying with him, Coleridge had an accident that forced him to stay at home. While his friends were out walking one evening, Coleridge composed this poem. It contrasts the landscapes he imagines his friends experiencing with the closer delights of the lime-tree bower in which he is sitting:

> 'Now my friends emerge
> Beneath the wide wide Heaven – and view again
> The many-steepled tract magnificent
> Of hilly fields and meadows, and the sea,
> With some fair bark, perhaps, whose sails light up
> The slip of smooth clear blue betwixt two Isles
> Or purple shadow!...

> ...A delight
> Comes sudden on my heart, and I am glad
> As I myself were there! Nor in this bower,
> This little lime-tree bower, have I not mark'd
> Much that hath sooth'd me. Pale beneath the blaze
> Hung the transparent foliage; and I watch'd
> Some broad and sunny leaf, and lov'd to see
> The shadow of the leaf and stem above
> Dappling its sunshine!...'

Keats was also fascinated by the natural world, but he often turned to the interior landscape of the mind in his poetry. His reaction to the mood of his times was not only to reject politics and industrialization, but to seek in poems such as 'Ode to Psyche' (1819) and 'Ode to a Nightingale' a Romantic and entirely interior dream landscape, a sensual world that did not exist in England or anywhere else. In 'Ode to a Nightingale'. Keats wrote about his mind escaping to a place where there is:

'...no light
Save what from heaven is with the breezes blown
Through verdurous glooms and winding mossy ways.'

Some modern critics have regarded Keats's brand of individualism as having its roots in his background: his liberal and progressive education, his youthful admiration for radical politics, and his Romantic idealism which, while despairing of the social conditions created by the Industrial Revolution, gave him the vision – like Blake – to see that it was necessary to believe in and aspire to an ideal world. Keats was an accomplished letter-writer and much of his thinking on poetry and his personal reactions to life around him can be found in these letters (which T.S. Eliot considered the 'most important ever written by any English poet'). Keats particularly disliked poetry which 'has a palpable design upon us...' and went on to say that 'Poetry should be... unobtrusive', that is, good poetry should be subtle. An aspect of his characteristically Romantic individualism is his suspicion of philosophical systems, saying that 'axioms in philosophy are not axioms until they are proved upon our pulses'.

For Keats, as for all Romantics, individual experience was all. He particularly admired what he called 'Negative Capability', which he defined in a letter to his brothers as 'when man is capable of being in uncertainties, Mysteries, doubts, without any irritable reaching after fact & reason...', in other words being satisfied with a non-rational response to the world around you. He considered that of all great poets, Shakespeare had this 'capability' in abundance, and implied that it was this ability to absorb and respond to the fullness of life, with all its inconsistencies, that gave Shakespeare the gift to create rounded, three-dimensional characters.

—SOME CONTEMPORARY— RESPONSES TO KEATS...

'One of the Cockney School of Poetry... It is a better and a wiser thing to be a starved apothecary than a starved poet; so back to the shop, Mr John...' (This was the reaction to Keats's Endymion *in the right-wing* Blackwood's Edinburgh Magazine *by the critic John Gibson Lockhart. It refers to the poet's relinquishing his trade as an apothecary to devote himself to poetry [see Biographical Glossary]. These comments so wounded Keats that he stopped writing for 18 months of his brief poetic career.)*

Like 'a pale flower by some sad maiden cherished...'
(Shelley)

...AND FROM LATER IN THE 19TH CENTURY

'One of the beginners of the Romantic movement, with all the extravagance and ignorance of his youth... His contemporaries, as Wordsworth, Byron, Shelley, and even Leigh Hunt, right or wrong, still concerned themselves with great causes, as liberty and religion; but he lived in mythology and fairyland the life of a dreamer.'
(Gerard Manley Hopkins)

B. R. Haydon (1786-1846)
Drawing of John Keats (1816)
The sensitivity of Keats is apparent in this contemporary sketch.
It is this kind of Romantic image that gave rise to the reputation
of poets as frail and consumptive.

37

Childhood

The Romantic period saw the development of interest in the experience of children and childhood. In 'Suspira De Profundis: The Affliction of Childhood' (published in *Blackwood's Edinburgh Magazine* 1845) Thomas De Quincy wrote of the traumatic effect of the death of his sister. But more often the Romantic poets wrote of the happy times of childhood, sometimes in contrast to adult cares, as in 'the happier hours' of William Lisle Bowles (1762-1851), who depicts a Winchester schoolboy wandering by the river in his sonnet 'To the River Itchen, near Winton' (1789); or Coleridge doing the same by his native Devon river in 'Sonnet V: To the River Otter' (c.1793). Coleridge was determined that his eldest son, Hartley would be formed by a free-spirited childhood, wandering:

> ...like a breeze
> By lakes and sandy shores, beneath the crags
> Of ancient mountain, and beneath the clouds...
> (from 'Frost at Midnight')

Wordsworth was acutely aware of the importance of childhood, and children's early experiences. 'Intimations of Immortality from Recollections of Early Childhood', a poem that confirmed his belief in the importance of childhood experience, mourned the passing of the visionary power of the child:

> 'There was a time when meadow, grove, and stream,
>   The earth, and every common sight,
>   To me did seem
>   Apparelled in celestial light,
> The glory and the freshness of the dream.
> It is not now as it hath been of yore;–
>   Turn wheresoe'er I may,
>   By night and day,
> The things which I have seen I now can see no more.'

Wordsworth often observed with fascination the naturalness of children, as in 'We are Seven' (1798) or some of the 'Lucy' poems, and, with an adult perspective, feared for the future of children.

The Americans

The American Revolution (see page 21) pointed the way toward a Romantic concept of individualism. In his draft for the American Declaration of Independence, Thomas Jefferson (1743-1826) wrote that all men were created 'equal and independent', and had a right to 'life, liberty and the pursuit of happiness'. This kind of sentiment was absolutely in line with Romantic thinking.

Romanticism in America picked up on the non-conformist and individual ways of doing things. The early Americans were Romantic in their belief that they had a unique sense of self, and that each individual's relationship with God was a personal one, needing no intermediary. There emerged in literature an archetypal American who was his own hero, living at the frontiers of an Eden-like American wilderness. James Fenimore Cooper (1789-1851) created such a figure in his series of *Leatherstocking Tales*, historical romances about a pioneer scout, Natty Bumppo, who, under various aliases such as 'Deer-slayer', 'Pathfinder' and 'Hawkeye', creates a living among the forests, mountains and lakes of upstate New York.

—'THE PIONEERS' (1823)— BY JAMES FENIMORE COOPER

In this story from Leatherstocking Tales, *Natty Bumppo is an old man who has seen a measure of so-called civilization come to his area of upper New York State. One of the central conflicts of the book is the individual's clash with the constraining hand of official institutions. Natty, whose nickname comes from the deerskin leggings he wears, falls foul of the law for killing a deer out of the newly established 'official' hunting season. He complains bitterly that, like the Native Americans, he kills only for need, food and clothing. By contrast, he watches the community indulge in the wholesale slaughter of pigeons for mere sport. At the end of the book he heads west, like Mark Twain's Huckleberry Finn, in order to escape the confines of civilization and to regain his individual freedom in the natural surroundings of the American wilderness.*

———————————

The individual against the backdrop of the grandeur of Nature is a repeated theme in American literature, nowhere more so than in the epic novel by Herman Melville (1819-91), *Moby Dick* (1851). In this novel the crew of a whaling ship is led into the wilderness by a mad, tyrannical leader, Captain Ahab, who is obsessed by his quest for Moby Dick, the white whale. Melville said, romantically and melodramatically, 'My book is woven of ships' cables and hawsers. A polar wind blows through it, and birds of prey hover over it.'

Transcendentalism was a specifically American school of philosophy, but it owed much to German Romanticism and to the English Lake District poets. The essential idea was a belief that God exists in all things in Nature, spiritually uniting them. Through their intuition, Transcendentalists came to understand their connection with and place within all things in creation. 'The currents of the Universal being circulate through me; I am a part or parcel of God' said Ralph Waldo Emerson (1803-82), a Unitarian minister from Concord, Massachusetts, who was much revered as the leading figure of the movement. Much in Transcendentalism was similar to Coleridge's sense of God as the 'Great Universal Teacher', or Wordsworth's 'Wisdom and Spirit of the Universe'.

Walt Whitman (1819-92), a prophetic poet in the mold of Blake, was influenced by Emerson to create a distinctive 'American' kind of verse, loose and free from traditional metrical constraint ('I am American, one of the roughs...' he wrote in his great epic poem *Leaves of Grass* (1856-92), which he worked on throughout his literary life). Whitman adopted what Coleridge had previously called an 'organic form', where the form of a work arises naturally out of the writer's subject and theme, growing and taking shape like a living organism, rather than being governed by a set of rules, as in 'mechanic form' (see Glossary of Terms). In his turning away from traditional modes of poetry, Whitman echoed the Wordsworth of the 1790s.

Henry David Thoreau (1817-62), a neighbor of Emerson, lived on his own in the woods and aspired to an ecological, non-materialist mode of living. He went further than Emerson by advocating civil disobedience as a protest against state interference in the lives of individuals. His rebellious spirit lived on into the 20th century through the Beat Generation, the civil rights movements, and the anti-Vietnam War protesters.

—*An American Dictionary of—*
the English Language
(2 volumes, 1828)

A typical idea of Romanticism was the perception of language as the sign of a unique culture. When a dominant culture seeks to suppress a minority culture, one of the things often done is to forbid the use of the minority tongue in schools, insisting that its own, supposedly superior, language is used. There was nothing Americans could do to escape the fact that English was the language they had inherited from Britain. However, Noah Webster (1758-1843) regarded British English as not always adapted to a country that was becoming composed of immigrants from increasingly varied ethnic backgrounds. Accordingly he set about compiling his dictionary for Americans, simplifying the chaotic spelling conventions of English and giving them greater logical coherence. In doing this he went some way toward establishing an American linguistic culture that was distinctively different from the mother country.

Romanticism and women

The Romantic period began to see changes in attitudes toward women, with regard to their political and social rights and also their status as writers and professionals. The process of change was a slow one: until 1871 a woman's property passed automatically to her husband when she married, and it was not until 1928 that women were allowed to vote in general elections in Britain. Nevertheless, the role of women as intellectuals and artists was established during the Romantic period, which led to an increasing recognition through the course of the 19th century of the wider part they had to play in public life.

In the 1770s Thomas Paine had published pamphlets in America advocating the emancipation of women. In 1792 Mary Wollstonecraft's *A Vindication of the Rights of Woman* appeared. She was part of a group of radical thinkers, which included Blake, who looked to the French Revolution to lead the way in liberating women, especially from subordination in marriage. Blake, who enjoyed a happy and well-adjusted relationship with his wife, Catherine, denounced the plight of women in *Visions of the Daughters of Albion* (1793); at one point he suggested to Catherine that they have an open marriage (that is, both were free to take other sexual partners from time to time), but she thought this was a bad idea and so, as he loved her, he dropped it.

Thomas Cole (1801-48)
Scene from Last of the Mohicans **(1827)**
Inspired by James Fenimore Cooper's Romantic novel, *The Last of the Mohicans* (1826; see page 39), Cole's painting captures the awesome grandeur and vastness of the American wilderness. The wild territory beyond the frontier was important to Cole and his fellow American Romantic painters. He once wrote that 'the wilderness is yet a fitting place to speak of God'.

Percy Shelley also advocated free love, believing that marriage enslaved women.

A reappraisal of the 'social' role of women coincided with a dramatic increase in the number of women who enjoyed careers as writers and in the number of educated women who wished to read their books. This demand coincided with the growth of circulating libraries (see page 20), which allowed easier access to their work and promoted literacy among their readers. The novel, in particular, became the form associated with female writing, partly because it was suited to describing the domestic environment and the conflicts of feeling and individual ideology that female writers and their readers knew well. Some of the early novelists were in fact well established in the publishing industry already by the 1770s and '80s: Maria Edgeworth (1767-1849) and Anna Laetitia Barbauld (1743-1825) wrote on a wide variety of topics including female education, the theories of Rousseau and the history of the novel, besides writing novels and poetry of their own. Ann Radcliffe (1764-1823) is best known for her Gothic novel *The Mysteries of Udolpho* (1794; see page 74), although she wrote a number of other romantic novels.

Most successful female writers had enjoyed a good education and came from wealthy or comfortably-off families. In such cases, education and charitable activity were nevertheless often the only public roles available to women, and so writing about these issues was a more fulfilling response to that role. Hannah More (1745-1833) was taught Latin, Spanish, Italian and French at a school run by her older sisters in Bristol, and went on to become a successful playwright in London society. However, her strong religious convictions led her to turn to religious and political writing, and she became an important figure in the campaign to end slavery and in the Sunday School movement.

The emphasis on the domestic, charitable and educational in women's writing reinforced to male readers and onlookers the idea that women's writing was inferior to that of male authors. In *Northanger Abbey* (written 1798, published 1818), Jane Austen breaks out of the narrative to comment on the way in which the novel is treated as a second-rate form: 'Although our productions [novels] have afforded more extensive and unaffected pleasure than those of any other literary corporation in the world, no species of composition has been so much decried. From pride, ignorance or fashion, our foes are almost as many as our readers.' However, she continues to justify the novel as the form of writing in which 'the greatest powers of the mind are displayed, in which the most thorough knowledge of human nature, the happiest delineation of its varieties, the liveliest effusions of wit and humour are conveyed to the world in the best chosen language.'

4. ECONOMIC AND SOCIAL CONTEXTS

The late 18th century was a time of rapid change in the living conditions of the people of Britain. The principal causes driving these changes were the so-called Agricultural and Industrial revolutions. It is important to realize that these terms were adopted some time after the events they describe. 'Revolution' was not a word toward which much of the 18th-century British public felt sympathetic, and these agricultural and industrial changes were not revolutions in the same political sense as the American or French revolutions. Instead, the terms are used to describe many different developments in different fields which took place at the same time, and which had a huge impact on the everyday lives of ordinary people.

The revolution in farming

During the 18th century, various developments in agriculture revolutionized farming methods. Some of these developments involved new inventions in farming equipment. For example, in the early 18th century a farmer called Jethro Tull (1674-1741) invented a mechanical seed drill that enabled seed to be sown evenly and correctly spaced, instead of by hand, which wasted seed. Tull's invention was the first step towards the mechanization of agriculture in Britain.

Other developments helped to improve farming practice. Also in the early 18th century, Viscount Charles Townshend (1674-1738), or 'Turnip Townshend' as he became known, began to experiment with new ways of rotating crops – that is, the practice of planting different crops in the same soil each year. He abandoned the traditional method of leaving a field fallow (unplanted) every three or four years in order allow the soil to recover. Instead he discovered that sowing turnips in the fourth year of the rotation cleaned the field, had no ill effects on the soil, and produced a crop that was useful for both human and animal consumption. This, in turn, meant that animals did not have to survive the winter half-starved, or be killed off and the meat salted. Another pioneer of the Agricultural Revolution was Robert Bakewell (1725-95). On his farm in Leicestershire, he experimented with breeding techniques to produce better quality cattle, sheep and horses. He was best known for raising sheep that provided not only wool, but also good-quality meat.

The advances of the Agricultural Revolution meant that farming became more efficient and profitable, and that both the quality and quantity of available food increased. However, the introduction of mechanization also meant that fewer people were needed to work on the land, and many former agricultural workers were forced to move to the rapidly expanding towns and cities to find work.

Enclosures

Another factor for change in the previously static nature of rural communities was the enclosure movement. Enclosure was a process by which landowners took over small plots of land and stretches of common land that were previously available to all and 'enclosed' these areas with hedges or walls to create large fields. This process had been taking place since medieval times, but it speeded up during the 18th century as wealthy farmers expanded their farms. Any landlord who wished to hedge and enclose common land for his own use had to put forward to Parliament a bill for enclosure, upon which local commissioners took over and decided upon the levels of compensation for those deprived of their rights. The decision almost always went in favor of the landlord, and by 1850 most of the agricultural land in England was enclosed.

Enclosure brought the economic benefit of greater efficiency, but the poor suffered. Many farmers of small plots were squeezed off their land, and the enclosure of common land meant that people had nowhere to graze their animals or to collect firewood. Arthur Young (1741-1820), a contemporary commentator on agriculture, wrote in *The Farmer's Tour through the East of England* (1771): 'The poor may say with truth, "Parliament may be tender of property; all I know is that I had a cow and an Act of Parliament has taken it away from me."' Enclosure increased the pressure for the poor to leave the country for employment in the new towns and cities. In his poem *The Deserted Village* (1770), Oliver Goldsmith saw the land as a place 'Where wealth accumulates, and men decay'. This poem is an elegy for a lost rural Britain, destroyed by enclosure and mechanization and the depopulation caused by the Agricultural and Industrial

— *RURAL RIDES* —

William Cobbett (1763-1835) was a radical activist who had a colorful career in the army, as a farmer and as a journalist. His best-known work is Rural Rides *(1830-3), essays based on his travels around England. These two extracts give a flavor of Cobbett's views on the effects of enclosures, and of the plight of industrial workers in the North of England:*

'I cannot quit Waltham Chase without observing, that I heard, last year, that a Bill was about to be petitioned for, to enclose that Chase! If the Chase be enclosed, the timber must be cut down young and old… Therefore, besides the sweeping away of two or three hundred cottages; besides plunging into ruin and misery all those numerous families, here is one of the finest pieces of timber-land in the whole kingdom, going to be cut up into miserable clay fields, for no earthly purpose but that of gratifying the stupid greed of those who think that they must gain, if they add to the breadth of their private fields.'

'Talk of vassals! Talk of villains! Talk of serfs! Are there any of these, or did feudal times ever see any of them, so debased, so absolutely slaves, as the poor creatures who, in the 'enlightened' North, are compelled to work fourteen hours in a day, in a heat of eighty-four degrees; and who are liable to punishment for looking out at a window of the factory!'

John Constable (1776-1837)
The Cornfield **(1826)**
Pictures such as this painting by Constable (see page 65)
represented for many the kind of rural idyll that was being lost in
the Industrial Revolution. Whether or not such an idealized
image of the countryside was founded in any kind of reality is
regarded by some as immaterial: Romanticism for such as Blake
was about the ideal, not the real.

revolutions. Much as, two decades later, Wordsworth mourned the disappearance of independent shepherds such as Michael, so Goldsmith went on to note that, whereas landowners may come and go:

'...a bold peasantry, their country's pride
When once destroyed, can never be supplied...'

The Industrial Revolution

The Industrial Revolution was born in Britain, later spreading to Europe and the United States. Just as in farming, the invention of new machines was a vital ingredient. The manufacture of cloth had long been an important industry in Britain, but the development of machines such as the spinning jenny (c.1764; by James Hargreaves c.1722-78) and the water frame (1769; by Richard Arkwright 1732-92) speeded up the processes of spinning and weaving. However, machines such as these needed a source of power. Wind and water were the traditional forces used to drive machinery, but the development of a practical steam engine during the 18th-century provided the regular source of power needed to drive the new manufacturing machines. It followed that if many of these machines were gathered together in one place – a mill or factory – then the manufacturing efficiency became even greater.

Steam power was generated by the burning of coal, and so new, deep coalpits were dug in areas such as South Wales and the Midlands regions of Britain. The development of new methods of smelting iron during the 18th century led to immensely stronger machines and structures, such as the world's first iron bridge (see page 19). Improvements in communications such as roads, canals, and later the railways assisted in the rapid distribution of raw products and cheap, mass-produced goods.

As a direct result of the changes created by the Agricultural and Industrial revolutions, thousands of people began to move from the countryside into the towns and cities, where they found more secure jobs and higher wages than those offered for work on the land. However, living conditions in these rapidly expanding towns and cities were often cramped and grim. New buildings were quickly erected to house the influx of workers, but they often lacked even the most basic amenities. In *A Vindication of the Rights of Man* (1790), Mary Wollstonecraft noted that 'in this great city [London] that proudly rears its head and boasts of its population and commerce, how much misery lurks in pestilent corners.' Similarly, Robert Southey wrote in his *Letters from England* (1807): 'The dwellings of the labouring manufacturers are in narrow streets and lanes, blocked up from lights and air... crowded together because every inch of land is of such value, that room for light and air cannot be afforded them...'.

Slum housing was not the only privation suffered by the industrial worker. Factory owners grew rich by demanding long hours for low wages, often employing children and women instead of men so that they could pay them less. There were, as yet, no laws to prevent long hours or to ensure that machines were safe. Yet there were well-intentioned owners, such as the Welsh businessman Robert Owen (1771-1858), who tried to make working conditions as good as possible. At his cotton mills in New Lanark, Scotland, he established a model community, with housing, a school, a village store, and the world's first day nursery for childcare.

Attitudes toward rural change

By the early 19th century Coleridge, Southey and Wordsworth had espoused what has been called a 'humanistic rural conservatism': they opposed the 'political economy' advocated by progressive economists of the time which, in general terms, put economic advantage above considerations of the traditional fabric of rural communities. Wordsworth expressed this fear – that the pursuit of profit was dehumanizing mankind – in a sonnet which begins:

'The world is too much with us; late and soon,
Getting and spending, we lay waste our powers;
Little we see in Nature that is ours;
We have given our hearts away, a sordid boon!'

As discussed on page 44, the latter half of the 18th century saw the breakdown of stable agricultural communities and a drift toward the cities for employment. For example, large numbers of agricultural laborers from Essex moved into London and settled in the East End – which rapidly became a slum area. In 'Holy Thursday II' (1794) Blake expressed the plight of the new urban poor in terms of the rurality they had recently lost:

'And their sun does never shine
And their fields are bleak and bare,
And their ways are fill'd with thorns;
It is eternal winter there.'

Admittedly, life in the countryside was hard: the increase in population and the unreliability of work led people to seek more permanent employment in the new towns. But at least rural communities tended to be relatively close-knit. In the towns people crowded together but, as Wordsworth pointed out in *The Prelude*, they often did not even know the names of their next-door neighbors:

'Above all, one thought
Baffled my understanding; how men lived
Even next-door neighbours, as we say, yet still
Strangers, not knowing each the other's name.'

The rural community spirit, so precious to Wordsworth, was lost in the towns and cities of the Industrial Revolution. One example that illustrates the closeness of the community in which Wordsworth lived with his sister Dorothy (1771-1855) and his wife Mary (1770-1859) was the Easedale tragedy, which happened in March 1808. Wordworth's favorite evening walk was to climb up along Sour Milk Gill, a spectacular waterfall especially after heavy rain, to Easedale Tarn, a peaceful small lake surrounded by mountains about three miles from his home in Grasmere. Along the way was a cottage – which still stands – in which lived George and Sarah Green and their six children. They were, said Wordsworth, 'the poorest people in the vale', but they were well-liked and respected, the children being 'the admiration of every Body for their innocence, affectionate dispositions, and good behaviour'. One day George and Sarah Green set off over the fells into Langdale to attend a sale. On their return a snowstorm set in. The Greens must have become disoriented, for they lost their way, fell down some steep crags, and perished. Dorothy explained in a letter that they:

'went to a sale in Langdale in the afternoon; and set off homewards in the evening, intending to cross the fells and descend just above their own cottage, a lonely dwelling in Easedale. They had left a daughter at home eleven years old, with the care of five brothers and sisters younger than herself, the youngest an infant at the breast. These dear helpless creatures sat up till 11 o'clock expecting their parents, and then went to bed thinking that they had stayed all night in Langdale because of the weather. All next day they continued to expect them, and on Monday morning one of the boys went to a house on the opposite side of the dale to borrow a cloak. On being asked for what purpose he replied that his sister was going to Langdale to 'lait [seek] their Folk' who had never come home. The man of the house started up, and said that they were lost; and immediately spread the alarm. As long as daylight lasted on that day, and on Monday and till Tuesday afternoon, all the men of Grasmere and many from Langdale were out upon the Fells. On Tuesday afternoon the bodies were found miserably mangled, having been cut by the crags. They were lying not above a quarter of a mile above a house in Langdale where their shrieks had been distinctly heard by two different persons who supposed that the shrieks came from some drunken people who had been at the sale. The bodies were brought home in a cart, and buried in one grave last Thursday. The poor children all the time they had been left by themselves suspected no evil; and as soon as it was known by others that their father and mother were missing the truth came upon them like a thunder-stroke.' (28 March 1808)

It is worth noting that so strongly knit was the rural community of the time that 'all the men of Grasmere' stopped work to look for the parents. Mary Wordsworth and other village women formed a committee to foster the children, the Wordsworths themselves taking in one of the daughters.

— LOCAL VOICES—

In the Romantic period the dominance enjoyed by London for well over a hundred years as the place where writers produced their work began to be challenged. Strong local voices were appearing far from London, none more so than the Scottish writer Robert Burns (1759-96) whose Poems, Chiefly in the Scottish Dialect *was published in Kilmarnock in 1786. Burns was admired by his fellow Romantics, and is still celebrated for his sympathetic view of the humblest aspects of nature (as in 'To a Mouse'), and for his upholding of the rights and freedoms of ordinary people (as in 'Love and Liberty'). Burns's fellow country-man from the Border country, Walter Scott, continued to put Scottish writing on the popular literary map with his highly successful* The Minstrelsy of the Scottish Border *(1802-03) and* The Lay of the Last Minstrel *(1805), and his verse romances* Marmion *(1808) and* The Lady of the Lake *(1810).*

Attitudes toward the commercial world

The Romantics saw the need to fight for identity and individuality against the anonymity of the production progress brought about by the coming of the machine. In *The Excursion*, Wordsworth wrote:

'Our life is turned
Out of her course, wherever man is made
An offering, or a sacrifice, a tool
Or implement, a passive thing employed
As a brute mean...'

Elsewhere in the same poem, Wordsworth describes the rapid growth of the new, industrial towns and cities:

'Meanwhile, at social Industry's command,
How quick, how vast an increase! From the germ
Of some poor hamlet, rapidly produced
Here a huge town, continuous and compact...
O'er which the smoke of unremitting fires
Hangs permanent, and plentiful as wreaths
Of vapour glittering in the morning sun...'

The Romantics opposed the dehumanizing growth of industrialization and commerce, and the brutalizing effect of dull, repetitive labor practices. They were hostile to the Utilitarian philosophies (see box) of Jeremy Bentham (1748-1832) and James Mill (1773-1836). However, these philosophies chimed in with the thinking of the Romantics insofar as they radically questioned previous ways of doing things. The Industrial Revolution brought great wealth to Britain, but the uneven distribution of this wealth was a source of bitterness to Romantics such as Southey and Shelley. Exploitation of labor was a fact of life both in the factories and mills, and in the countryside. In his poem 'Song to the Men of England' (1819), Shelley is typically forthright in his condemnation of such exploitation:

> 'Men of England, wherefore plough
> For the lords who lay ye low?
> Wherefore weave with toil and care
> The rich robes your tyrants wear?
>
> Wherefore feed, and clothe, and save,
> From the cradle to the grave,
> Those ungrateful drones who would
> Drain your sweat – nay, drink your blood?'

— UTILITARIANISM—

The doctrine of Utilitarianism was developed by the philosopher Jeremy Bentham and taken up in the next generation by the economist John Stuart Mill (1806-73), son of James (see main text), and others. In general, Utilitarianism valued things only by their strict usefulness to the greatest number of people. Hence literature and other products of the imagination were considered of little practical use. The emotionally crippling effects of Utilitarianism were attacked by the novelist Charles Dickens (1812-70) in Hard Times *(1845), in which the loveless merchant, Thomas Gradgrind, values facts and rejects imagination (which Dickens called 'Fancy'). John Stuart Mill described in his* Autobiography *(1873) such effects in his own upbringing. In 1826 he underwent a mental crisis, but found rescue and solace in the poetry of Wordsworth and Coleridge. He records the spiritual awakening he experienced upon first reading their poetry, Wordsworth in particular bringing him, in his own words, 'a greatly increased interest in the common feelings and common destiny of human beings', and leading him to modify his ingrained Utilitarian principles. Oscar Wilde's notion of one who 'knows the price of everything and the value of nothing' may be taken as a cynic's definition of a Utilitarian.*

Child labor

Another area of exploitation was the use of children for cheap labor. The practice of hiring young children was commonplace, and nobody expressed greater horror at the abuse of their innocence than Blake. Their work in factories, mills, mines and other places was often carried out in appalling conditions, and was still a subject of attack by Dickens a generation after Blake's famous portrayal of the plight of the little chimney sweeps. During the 19th century the House of Commons on many occasions passed bills designed to improve the conditions of chimney sweeps, but their passage into law was blocked by the House of Lords. The 'apprenticing' of children as young as four was virtual slavery:

> 'My father sold me while yet my tongue
> Could scarcely cry 'weep' 'weep' 'weep' 'weep'!
> So your chimneys I sweep and in soot I sleep.'
> (from 'The Chimney Sweeper I' in *Songs of Innocence*)

In this poem, the boy is so young that his lisping attempt at advertising his trade as 'sweep' comes out as 'weep', an ironic comment on the misery of his situation. Blake emphasized the neglect by adults of children in another poem entitled 'The Chimney Sweeper' (in *Songs of Experience*). Here the parents of the 'little black thing among the snow' have dressed him in 'clothes of death' and then abandoned him while they go off to church in order to:

> 'Praise God and his priest and king
> Who make up a Heaven of our misery.'

The anti-establishment feelings expressed by Blake in this poem were the same as those being expressed in revolutionary France and among radical groups in London, and echo down three decades to Shelley's 'The Mask of Anarchy' (see page 30). Yet Blake always held on to his idealistic vision that things could change and that salvation was possible. In 'The Chimney Sweeper I' he offered the possibility, however fantastic, of an angel setting free all the little chimney sweeps. And in 'Holy Thursday II' he promised the building of a land of plenty for all:

> 'For where-e'er the sun does shine,
> And where-e'er the rain does fall,
> Babe can never hunger there,
> Nor poverty the mind appal.'

Wordsworth, too, recorded his concern for the plight of child laborers in his poetry. Children were small and nimble, and therefore used for such jobs as operating trapdoors and hauling coal in cramped tunnels in the mines, and sweeping waste from beneath the machines in cotton mills. In *The Excursion* Wordsworth paints a touching 'Picture of a child employed in a Cotton-mill' whose 'holiday of childhood' has been cruelly cut short by the slavery of such work:

> 'His raiment, whitened o'er with cotton-flakes
> Or locks of wool, announces whence he comes.
> Creeping his gait and cowering, his lip pale,
> His respiration quick and audible...'

Here, the poet describes the physical damage done to the boy – the pallor and the difficulties in breathing – but he is also concerned with the damage to the boy's mind and soul by his incarceration in the mill when he should be experiencing the 'forms of nature':

'He is a slave to whom release
   comes not,
And cannot come. The boy where'er
   he turns,
Is still a prisoner; when the wind is
   up
Among the clouds, and roars through
   the ancient woods;
Or when the sun is shining in the
   east,
Quiet and calm...'

Slavery

During the Romantic period, opposition to the slave trade was growing in Britain. The slave trade between West Africa and the Americas had started in the 16th century, and many people in ports such as Liverpool and Bristol had become wealthy on the proceeds. In 1787, the Society for the Abolition of the Slave Trade was founded in Britain by the anti-slavery campaigners William Wilberforce (1759-1833), Thomas Clarkson (1760-1846) and Granville Sharp (1735-1813), and the following year an Act of Parliament limited the number of black slaves who could be transported from Africa to the British Caribbean colonies. However, a bill in 1791 to abolish the slave trade was defeated, prompting the poet Anna Laetitia Barbauld to write a heartfelt 'Epistle' to William Wilberforce:

Cease, Wilberforce, to urge thy
   generous aim!
Thy Country knows the sin, and
   stands the shame!
The Preacher, Poet, Senator in vain
Has rattled in her sight the Negro's
   chain;
With his deep groans assail'd her
   startled ear,
And rent the veil that hid his constant
   tear;

— 'THE LITTLE BLACK BOY' —

Blake wrote the following poem in 1789, during a period when concern about the evils of slavery was growing among the more liberal-minded in Britain. One of the engravings that accompanies the poem shows the little African boy with his mother, under the scorching African sun (see illustration opposite). The poem emphasizes the little boy's closeness to God:

'My mother bore me in the southern wild,
And I am black, but O! my soul is white;
White as an angel is the English child,
But I am black, as if bereav'd of light.

My mother taught me underneath a tree,
And sitting down before the heat of day,
She took me on her lap and kissed me,
And pointing to the east, began to say:

"Look on the rising sun: there God does live,
And gives his light, and gives his heat away;
And flowers and trees and beasts and men receive
Comfort in morning, joy in the noonday.

And we are put on earth a little space,
That we may learn to bear the beams of love;
And these black bodies and this sunburnt face
Is but a cloud, and like a shady grove.

For when our souls have learn'd the heat to bear,
The cloud will vanish; we shall hear his voice,
Saying: 'Come out from the grove, my love and care,
And round my golden tent like lambs rejoice.' "

Thus did my mother say, and kissed me;
And thus I say to little English boy,
When I from black and he from white cloud free,
And round the tent of God like lambs we joy,

I'll shade him from the heat, till he can bear
To lean in joy upon our father's knee;
And then I'll stand and stroke his silver hair,
And be like him, and he will then love me.'

William Blake (1757-1827)
'The Little Black Boy' *Songs of Innocence*
and of Experience **1789 and 1794**

Blake printed his own writings by engraving them, using a method of relief etching of his own invention: he reversed the usual method, eroding everything except the words and lines that he wished to be reproduced, and leaving them proud on the plate. He surrounded his writings with illustrations that he colored by hand.

Forc'd her averted eyes his stripes to scan,
Beneath the bloody scourge laid bare the man,
Claimed Pity's tear, urged Conscience' strong controul,
And flash'd conviction on her shrinking soul.

Other writers who also contributed to the abolitionist cause
included the poet Ann Yearsley (1756-1806) ('A Poem on the
Inhumanity of the Slave Trade' 1788), Hannah More (*The Sorrows
of Yamba* c.1795) and Southey (*To the Genius of Africa* 1797;
various sonnets in *Poems* 1797; *The Sailor Who had Served in the
Slave-Trade* 1799). Like many of his contemporary abolitionists,
Southey also advised others not to put sugar in tea as it was a
product of slave labor. The British slave trade was abolished in
1807, to the approval of Wordsworth, who wrote a sonnet to
Thomas Clarkson to mark the passing of the Bill. It ends:

'The blood-stained Writing is for ever torn;
And thou henceforth wilt have a good man's calm.
A great man's happiness; the zeal shall find
Repose at length, firm friend of humankind!'

Slavery itself was finally outlawed in the British Empire in 1833.

Attitudes toward the poor

Wordsworth's friends and contemporaries thought him highly
eccentric in his desire to observe and record in poetry the ordinary
and the common, both in subject matter and style. In the *Lyrical
Ballads* the 28-year-old poet used incidents involving the aged, the
poor, beggars, and vagrants, exploring relationships between people
– especially parents and children – and their environment.
Wordsworth had a genuine interest in these people, and believed
that he could learn from them. He also hoped to draw attention to
the plight of some of the poorest people in society through his
poetry. Sometimes his subjects were badly damaged, mentally or
physically, by their ordeals. The socially dispossessed who wander
across the pages of Wordsworth and some of the other Romantic
poets had sometimes suffered the effects of the Napoleonic Wars,
as in Wordsworth's 'Old Man Travelling' (1798). In this poem, the
poet closely observes an old man:

'I asked him whither he was bound, and what
The object of his journey; he replied
"Sir! I am going many miles to take
A last leave of my son, a mariner,
Who from a sea-fight hath been brought to Falmouth
And there is dying in the hospital."'

In 'The Old Cumberland Beggar' (1800), Wordsworth put forward the notion that the poor were useful to society because they inspired benevolence. He prefixed this note to the poem: 'The class of beggars to which the old man here described belongs will probably soon be extinct. It consisted of poor and, mostly, old and infirm persons, who confined themselves to a stated round in their neighbourhood, and had certain fixed days on which, at different houses, they regularly received alms, sometimes of money, but mostly in provisions'. He claimed that as a child he had been morally improved by witnessing such acts of charity, but that 'the political economists were about that time beginning their war on mendicity [begging] in all its forms, and, by implication if not directly, on almsgiving also':

> 'He travels on, a solitary Man,
> So helpless in appearance, that from him
> The sauntering Horseman throws not with a slack
> And careless hand his alms upon the ground,
> But stops, – that he may safely lodge the coin
> Within the old Man's hat; nor quits him so,
> But still, when he has given his horse the rein,
> Watches the aged Beggar with a look
> Sidelong, and half-reverted. She who tends
> The toll-gate, when in summer at her door
> She turns her wheel, if on the road she sees
> The aged Beggar coming, quits her work,...
> But deem not this Man useless. – Statesmen! ye
> Who are so restless in your wisdom, ye
> Who have a broom still ready in your hands
> To rid the world of nuisances; ye proud,
> Heart-swoln, while in your pride ye contemplate
> Your talents, power, or wisdom, deem him not
> A burden of the earth! 'Tis Nature's law
> That none, the meanest of created things,
> Of forms created the most vile and brute,
> The dullest or most noxious, should exist
> Divorced from good...
>   While from door to door,
> This old Man creeps, the villagers in him
> Behold a record which together binds
> Past deeds and offices of charity,
> Else unremembered, and so keeps alive
> The kindly mood in hearts which lapse of years,
> And that half-wisdom half-experience gives,
> Make slow to feel, and by sure steps resign
> To selfishness and cold oblivious cares,

Among the farms and solitary huts,
Hamlets and thinly-scattered villages,
Where'er the aged Beggar takes his rounds,
The mild necessity of use compels
The acts of love; and habit does the work
Of reason; yet prepares that after-joy
Which reason cherishes. And thus the soul,
By that sweet taste of pleasure unpursued,
Doth find herself insensibly disposed
To virtue and true goodness.'

Wordsworth was not here defending poverty. His view was that people such as the old beggar had an important function in society in inspiring charity, and he condemned those 'statesmen' who would see the beggar only as a public nuisance to be removed to the workhouse. He recognized the beggar's place in Nature, and that, in Blake's words 'Every thing that lives is holy' no matter how poor or lowly it may appear. Blake himself concludes his poem 'Holy Thursday I (Innocence)' (1794) with 'cherish pity, lest you drive an angel from your door'; yet, ambivalently, at the beginning of 'The Human Image' (1794, sometimes called 'The Human Abstract') he mocks the notion, ironically implying that charity is something that simply makes the doer feel good, and is no excuse for the smug acceptance of poverty:

'Pity would be no more
If we did not make somebody poor;
And Mercy no more could be
If all were as happy as we.'

Education and the Romantic imagination

Education was for many Romantics the way forward, and some of their ideas were taken from Rousseau (see page 12). A system of national state religious education was advanced by Wordsworth in *The Excursion* as the only way to instill moral values into the rural and urban poor – however, it was not until 1870 that an Education Bill introduced schooling for all, regardless of wealth. Mary Wollstonecraft, the novelist Maria Edgeworth, and Blake all wrote about the need for better education for women (see box page 57). But whatever their view about formal education, both Coleridge and Wordsworth clung to the idea that sometimes the best education happened in natural surroundings when perhaps the recipient was not aware of learning. Wordsworth, who had a very good education at Hawkshead Grammar School and St John's College, Cambridge University, nevertheless claimed that:

'One impulse from a vernal wood
May teach you more of man,
Of moral evil and of good
Than all the sages can.'
(from 'The Tables Turned')

He saw that much formal education was committed to filling pupils full of knowledge, redundant when unaccompanied by understanding. The school pupil:

'Can string you names of districts, cities, towns
The whole world over...
Meanwhile old Grandam Earth is grieved to find
The playthings which her love designed for him
Unthought of...'
(from 'The Five-Book Prelude' 1804)

Similarly well-educated, Coleridge felt that his imagination was suppressed at Christ's Hospital School in London. In 'Frost at Midnight' he referred to 'cloisters dim', and wished for his own son an education wandering 'like a breeze' within hearing of God's 'eternal language' in the wild countryside. He remembered walking as a child in Devon under a starry sky while his father pointed upwards and taught him about the universe. In a letter to his friend and supporter Thomas Poole (1797), Coleridge wrote, 'Should children be permitted to read romances, and relations of giants and magicians and genii? I know all that has been said against it, but I have formed my faith in the affirmative... I have known some who have been *rationally* educated, as it is styled. They were marked by a microscopic acuteness, but when they looked at great things, all became a blank and they saw nothing.'

— MARY WOLLSTONECRAFT —
ON THE EDUCATION OF WOMEN

Widely regarded as the founder of modern feminism, Mary Wollstonecraft wrote prolifically on many moral issues, including the limited nature of women's education. The following is an extract from her A Vindication of the Rights of Woman:

'*Many are the causes that, in the present corrupt state of society, contribute to enslave women by cramping their understandings... This contempt of the understanding in early life has more baneful consequences than is commonly supposed, for the little knowledge which women of strong minds attain is, from various circumstances, of a more desultory kind than the knowledge of men, and it is acquired more by sheer observations on real life than from comparing what has been individually observed with the results of experience generalised by speculation. Led by their dependant situation and domestic employments more into society, what they learn is rather by snatches; and as learning is with them, in general, only a secondary thing, they do not pursue any one branch with that persevering ardour necessary to give vigour to the faculties and clearness to the judgement.*

In the present state of society, a little learning is required to support the character of a gentleman, and boys are obliged to submit to a few years of discipline. But in the education of women, the cultivation of the understanding is always subordinate to the acquirement of some corporeal accomplishment...'

_____

5. PAINTING, MUSIC AND THEATRE

In much the same way as the French Revolution in 1789 meant that the old political and social certainties could no longer be counted on, so in art at around the same time agreed opinion began to break down as to what constituted beauty and taste – and even art itself. Likewise in music, the appearance of the first modern pianoforte in 1780 meant that the precision of the harpsichord gave way to a greater variety of tone and volume, allowing a pianist to bring more individual interpretation and Romantic passion to a piece of music. In architecture, the style laid down by the Italian Andrea Palladio (1508-80), and accepted in the Age of Reason as the 'correct' one for an elegant building, began to be questioned. When Horace Walpole, author of the first Gothic novel (see page 73), decided to redesign his house at Strawberry Hill, his taste for the individual and Romantic led him to create a building inspired by medieval Gothic castles. This 'Gothic revival' gathered pace during the 19th century across Europe, but during the late 18th and early 19th centuries a parallel movement saw architects rejecting Roman neo-Classical and looking to the lines of Classical Greek architecture, especially for great public buildings. In France, the tradition of the Baroque and Rococo (see Glossary of Terms) builders and decorators, identified with the castles and châteaux of royalty and aristocrats, was swept away by the revolutionaries who saw themselves as free citizens of a new era.

Painting

Art in Britain during the second half of the 18th century was dominated by Sir Joshua Reynolds (1723-92). He was a well-known and accomplished portrait artist who painted many of the most important people of his day. As part of his training he had spent some time in Italy, studying the great masters of the 16th and 17th centuries, such as Raphael and Titian, and these studies colored his whole approach to art. In the face of the growing trend toward individuality and breaking with tradition, Reynolds urged young artists to follow his example by examining the works of the great masters in order to understand their styles and techniques, and to copy their subject matter.

In 1768, the Royal Academy of Arts was founded in London and Reynolds became its first President. The aim of the Academy was to raise the status of artists and establish sound systems of training. To these ends, the Academy laid down what an artist should paint, and the style in which the subject should be painted. Reynolds himself gave a series of 15 annual lectures, known as

Discourses, which established the rules and theories that he considered necessary for the production of great art. The subject matter considered appropriate for an artist was very much taken for granted: scenes from the Bible, the lives of the saints, Classical mythology. Rarely did artists paint a scene from romance, history or contemporary life. Landscapes, so important to many Romantics, were not considered to offer sufficiently lofty or dignified subject matter for great art.

Nevertheless, Reynolds foresaw that these grand traditions in painting were in danger. During the late 18th century, assumptions about what was acceptable in art began to change – especially in France during the Revolution. A new emphasis on feeling and emotion meant that artists felt released to paint anything that appealed to their imaginations, whether a scene from Shakespeare, from recent history or, as with *The Death of Marat* (1793) by Jacques Louis David (1748-1825), an up-to-the minute depiction of a contemporary event (the murder of the French revolutionary Jacobin leader, Jean Paul Marat, by a Girondin sympathiser, Charlotte Corday, in 1793). Further afield, an artist such as the American John Singleton Copley (1737-1815) fell under none of the traditional constraints of the Old World. He looked for subjects from England's past, and there was a Romanticism in his painting which is comparable to the Gothic revival in architecture. His painting of *Charles I demanding the surrender of the five impeached members of the House of Commons* (1785) was considered to be shocking in its general nature as a scene from relatively recent history, but also because it depicted the defying of a monarch.

In Spain, Francisco Goya (1746-1828) also asserted his independence from past conventions, and in many ways he epitomizes the break with tradition by which artists felt free to depict on paper their private thoughts and visions in the same way as poets. Goya's paintings and prints are sometimes not even depictions of 'real' subjects, but are fantastic evocations from his imagination – witches, giants and apparitions that inhabit a world of the Gothic sub-conscious. One of the best-known of this type is *The Giant* (c.1818), which depicts a huge, naked giant sitting at the edge of the world, dwarfing the landscape and half-turning toward the viewer.

William Blake

Above all it is Blake, as both poet and artist, who embodied the break with tradition. He was a student at the Royal Academy for a time, but he disliked the 'official' art of Reynolds that was taught at the Academy. He rejected the domination of the Classical style, and the notion advanced by the Academy that painting was best learned by copying the work of the masters of the past. Blake considered the art world both materialistic and hypocritical, and he assigned much of the blame for this state of affairs to Reynolds. He owned a copy of Reynold's *Discourses,* which he covered with his own angry comments, including, on the title page, his opinion of the President of the Academy: 'This Man was Hired to Depress Art'. Blake was not interested in strict representational 'correctness' but was more concerned with bringing out imaginatively what an experience meant to him. In this Blake is characteristically Romantic, believing in the centrality of the imagination, and that an artist must reject the past and find his own way of doing things from within himself. He said, 'I must create my own system or be enslaved by another man's.'

In Blake's watercolor etching *The Ancient of Days* (1794), God is seen planning the world using a pair of compasses (see the illustration of Newton using compasses on page 7). This painting is inspired by two things: the following passage from the Bible, 'The Lord... set a compass on the face of the depths: when He established the clouds above: when He strengthened the fountains of the deep' (Proverbs viii), and secondly by the images of God painted by the Italian painter Michelangelo, whom Blake admired. Blake abhorred established, organized religion and, since he regarded the world as bad, the creator of that world was bad also. His picture depicts God much as he had depicted Isaac Newton: a cold, vengeful figure, devoid of warmth and feeling.

Blake's contemporaries thought him at best a harmless crank, at worst a madman. Wordsworth said of Blake: 'There was no doubt that this poor man was mad, but there is something in the madness of this man which interests me more than the sanity of Lord Byron and Walter Scott.' And there were some at the time who revered him. Samuel Palmer (1805-81) was a leading artist in a group that called themselves the Ancients. Members of the Ancients espoused the past as an inspiration for their works, in much the same way that in literature Blake looked back to Geoffrey Chaucer, Edmund Spenser and John Milton. However, Palmer was one of

— BLAKE THE ARTIST—

Blake served his apprenticeship to an engraver, James Basire, before entering the Royal Academy Schools to study engraving further. (Engraving is the process of cutting a design into a block of wood or metal and taking prints from this block.) Blake exhibited some of his work at the Academy, but he did not agree with its methods of teaching (see main text) and seems to have attended the Schools irregularly. In 1787, one of Blake's brothers, Robert, died of consumption. Blake claimed that, not long after his death, Robert appeared to him in a vision and showed him a particular method of engraving. The inspiration of this vision led Blake to engrave both a poem and its illustration together onto the same plate, allowing him to publish his poetry without 'the expense of letter-press'. Blake produced the first works using this method in 1788, but probably the most well-known are the poems and illustrations contained in the Songs of Innocence and of Experience *(see illustration page 53). Blake became extremely accomplished at mirror-writing his poetry directly onto the metal plate — necessary for the writing on the print to appear the right way around — as is recorded by a contemporary painter and friend of Blake's, John Linnell:*

'The most extraordinary facility seems to have been attained by Blake in writing backwards & that with a brush dipped in a glutinous liquid for the writing is in many instances highly ornamental & varied in character as may be seen in his Songs of Innocence*...'*

———————————

the very few who admired Blake and, although the Pre-Raphaelite painter Dante Gabriel Rossetti (1828-82) championed Blake, it was not until the mid-20th century that his significance as a Romantic was truly recognized.

The sublime and the picturesque

In 1757, the statesman and philosopher Edmund Burke published an essay entitled *A Philosophical Enquiry into the Origin of our Ideas of the Sublime and the Beautiful*. This work was to have a profound influence on the way in which artists, poets and others viewed the natural world. The idea of the 'sublime' was associated with anything that induced feelings of awe, terror and wonder, such as the dramatic, soaring mountain scenery that is found in the Alps. Burke was one of the first people to identify the power of 'obscurity', that is, 'dark, confused, uncertain images' which work on the imagination through their suggestiveness and 'form… grander passions than those which are more clear and determinate'. This concept was a marked contrast to the emphasis on clarity and precision that held sway during the Age of Reason (see page 5).

The artist who summed up all the elements of the sublime in his art was an Italian, Salvator Rosa (1615-73). Although he was working at the same time as Claude Lorrain (1600-82) and Nicolas Poussin (1594-1665) (see page 64), he produced paintings of wild and savage landscapes, quite different from the Classically influenced work of the two French painters. For 18th-century artists and writers, Rosa was closely associated with ideas of the sublime – so much so that when Horace Walpole crossed the Alps in 1739, he is said to have exclaimed: 'Precipices, mountains, torrents, wolves, rumblings – Salvator Rosa!'. Aspects of the sublime are very obvious in Gothic literature (see Chapter 6), but they also have a place in the work of the Romantic poets. In *The Prelude*, Wordsworth describes a walking tour of the Alps, undertaken while he was a student at Cambridge University. On 17 August 1790, Wordsworth and a companion crossed the Simplon Pass. Fifteen years later, he evoked his feelings about their experiences, using the language of the sublime in great poetry:

> 'Downwards we hurried fast,
> And, with the half-shaped road which we had missed,
> Entered a narrow chasm. The brook and road
> Were fellow-travellers in this gloomy strait,
> And with them did we journey several hours
> At a slow pace. The immeasurable height
> Of woods decaying, never to be decayed,
> The stationary blasts of waterfalls,
> And, in the narrow rent at every turn

Winds thwarting winds, bewildered and forlorn,
The torrents shooting out from the clear blue sky,
The rocks that muttered close upon our ears,
Black drizzling crags that spake by the way-side
As if a voice were in them, the sick sight
And giddy prospect of the raving stream,
The unfettered clouds and region of the Heavens,
Tumult and peace, the darkness and the light –
Were all like workings of one mind, the features
Of the same face, blossoms upon one tree;
Characters of the great Apocalypse,
The types and symbols of Eternity,
Of first, and last, and midst, and without end.'

Similarly, Shelley was inspired by a tour of the Alps in 1816. In his poem 'Mont Blanc' (1816) he, too, is moved to 'grander passions' by the drama of his surroundings (see also the extract from one of Shelley's letters on page 78):

'Thus thou, Ravine of Arve – dark, deep Ravine –
Thou many-coloured, many-voiced vale,
Over whose pines, and crags, and caverns sail
Fast cloud-shadows and sunbeams: awful scene.
Where Power in likeness of the Arve comes down
From the ice-gulfs that gird his secret throne,
Bursting through these dark mountains like the flame
Of lightning through the tempest; – thou dost lie,
Thy giant brood of pines around thee clinging,
Children of elder time, in whose devotion
The chainless winds still come and ever came
To drink their odours, and their mighty swinging
To hear – an old and solemn harmony...'

During the 18th century, the category of the sublime acquired a companion term – the picturesque. The picturesque was seen as a distinct concept because it was used to describe landscapes which did not necessarily inspire awe or terror, but which were full of variety and interest, appealing to the viewer's eye. Thus the picturesque could refer to a rural scene which to the viewer took on an idyllic simple beauty, or to the wild and remote. The picturesque was most clearly defined by Reverend William Gilpin (1724-1804), who published many accounts of his tours through Britain. According to Gilpin, the picturesque was essentially a painterly concept, allowing the viewer to assess a real landscape as if he or she were looking at a painting.

John Robert Cozens (1752-c.99)
Between Chamonix and Martigny (c.1778)

For many Romantics the soaring snow-clad mountains of the
Alps were a fascination. They represented the wild, remote,
desolate places to which writers from Rousseau to Mary and
Percy Shelley were attracted. It is in the mountains above
Chamonix, the 'glorious presence-chamber of imperial Nature',
that a meeting takes place between creator and creature in
Frankenstein (see page 78).

The seeking out of the picturesque became almost a cult in the 18th century. Parties sometimes travelled many miles in their carriages, and then walked over difficult terrain, in order to sit and admire a waterfall, a lake vista or mountain scenery which was deemed to be 'picturesque'. Gilpin defined 'picturesque travel' in the second essay from his best-selling *Three Essays on Picturesque Beauty* (1792): 'Its object is beauty of every kind, which either art, or nature can produce: but it is chiefly that species of beauty, which we have endeavoured to characterize in the preceding essay under the name of picturesque. This great object we pursue through the scenery of nature. We seek it among all the ingredients of landscape – trees – rocks – broken-grounds – woods – rivers – lakes – plains – vallies – mountains – and distances. These objects in themselves produce infinite variety. No two rocks, or trees are exactly the same. They are varied, a second time, by combination; and almost as much, a third time, by different lights, and shades, and other aerial effects...'

Jane Austen poked fun at the vogue for the picturesque in her novel *Northanger Abbey* when the highly fashionable Henry Tilney instructs the naïve heroine of the book, Catherine Morland, on how to look at a landscape in a picturesque manner: 'He talked of fore-grounds, distances, and second distances – side-screens and perspectives – lights and shades; and Catherine was so hopeful a scholar, that when they gained the top of Beechen Cliff, she voluntarily rejected the whole city of Bath, as unworthy to make part of a landscape.'

Elements of the picturesque were also woven into the works of poets and writers such as Addison, Pope, Thomas Gray (1716-71), and later on into the Gothic stories and novels of Sir Walter Scott. The picturesque is related to Romanticism, although some say that it a superficial manifestation of the true Romantic's deeper responses to the power of Nature.

Landscape painting

Landscape painting was one branch of art that particularly benefited from the Romantic drive toward freedom of individual expression. Very broadly, over the previous century or so artists had moved from a Classical depiction of nature, which was largely imaginary and idealized, to a desire to capture what they saw before them – and their individual response to what they saw. The Classical liking for pure lines and careful design, which appealed to the intellect, gave way to color, tonal contrast, and a stimulation through visual excitement. Yet painters in the Classical style such as Nicolas Poussin and Claude Lorrain had some influence upon the later Romantics, Turner particularly acknowledging his debt to Lorrain. Under the brushes of Romantic painters, the important thing was to convey through the painting an actual scene or event and how the artist himself reacted to it. This is the equivalent in art to what Wordsworth was doing in poetry in *Tintern Abbey* (see box).

The two most important Romantic artists in this respect were J.M.W. Turner (1775-1851) and John Constable (1776-1837). Although he was influenced by earlier landscape painters such as Claude Lorrain, Constable wanted to paint what he saw with his own eyes, not view landscape through the eyes of the masters of the past: the truth as he saw it was all important (see illustration page 45). Just as Romantic poets, especially Wordsworth, Shelley and Byron, often focus upon clouds and the sky as metaphors for Romantic freedom, so the sky is important in Constable's paintings. Constable said that for him, the sky was 'the key note, the standard scale, and the chief organ of sentiment...', and he was as interested in effects of light and atmosphere as in the details of the landscape. However, he had no wish to shock his audience into seeing the world in a new way as did Turner, whose work is deliberately arresting, full of daring lighting effects, movement and the wild, Romantic grandeur of Nature.

It is telling to compare Turner's *Battle of Trafalgar* paintings (1806 and 1824), *The Fighting Temeraire* (1838) or *Snow storm* (1842) with many a 17th- or 18th-century picture of ships. Earlier pictures show ships in accurate detail; Turner's ships are impressionistic hulks. What Turner makes the viewer feel is all important: detailed representation is immaterial. The ship is characteristically alone, a solitary Romantic battling alone in the universe to find a way through. Likewise in *Rain, Steam and Speed* (1844) (see illustration page 67) the railway engine (and the hare racing along in front of it) give the

— 'TINTERN ABBEY' —

The following lines are the opening of 'Lines Written a Few Miles above Tintern Abbey, on Revisiting the Banks of the Wye During a Tour, 13 July 1798'. Several aspects of Wordsworth's description indicate a new, Romantic attitude toward landscape. First, Tintern Abbey was in Wordsworth's day a well-known beauty spot, and one might have expected him to situate his reflections there; but he deliberately places himself a few miles upstream. Secondly, and more important, he does not try to depict in words the landscape in any detail, but merely gives an impression of the dominant features: the important thing is what the landscape means to him, its personal associations, its atmosphere, the emotional response the scene evokes in him as an individual — not any 'accurate' recording of the landscape's beauty. Indeed, the whole thrust of the poem is a meditation on how Wordsworth's feelings and reactions differ from how they were when he previously visited five years before, notwithstanding the fact that the landscape itself has not altered:

'Five years have passed; five summers, with the length
Of five long winters! And again I hear
These waters, rolling from their mountain springs
With a sweet inland murmur. Once again
Do I behold these steep and lofty cliffs,
Which on a wild secluded scene impress
Thoughts of more deep seclusion, and connect
The landscape with the quiet of the sky.
The day is come when I again repose
Here, under this dark sycamore, and view
These plots of cottage-ground, these orchard-tufts,
Which, at this season, with their unripe fruits,
Among the woods and copses lose themselves,
Nor, with their green and simple hue, disturb
The wild green landscape. Once again I see
These hedgerows — hardly hedgerows, little lines
Of sportive wood run wild; these pastoral farms
Green to the very door; and wreaths of smoke
Sent up in silence from among the trees...'

viewer a vivid feeling of the impression created by the engine (and the hare) and not an accurate presentation of detail. Turner's painting invites comparison with Shelley's poetry, especially in its brilliant lighting effects: it is an interesting exercise to look at a Turner painting and then read some lines from, for example, Shelley's 'The Cloud' (1820) or 'To a Skylark'. Turner shows Nature reflecting and expressing Man's emotions, not as an external feature separate and outside Man, to be observed coldly and recorded precisely. Similarly, in 'The Cloud', the poet personalizes the cloud (see box).

In the same way, painters in Europe such as the German Caspar David Friedrich (1774-1840) were capturing the spirit of the Romantic Age. Widely regarded as the greatest of the German Romantic artists, Friedrich was a lonely figure who gave up his life to creating on canvas individual perspectives of landscape which were usually melancholy and Gothic in their mysteriousness. He was never happier than when contemplating in solitude the rugged landscapes of his native part of Germany (see cover picture). The French painter Eugène Delacroix (1798-1863) (see illustration page 25) also developed into an archetypally Romantic painter in his use of space, movement and bright colors, creating what he called 'the musical part of painting'. These painters foreshadowed the French Impressionists of the later 19th century who, like Wordsworth's writing in 'Tintern Abbey', no longer tried to paint landscape and Nature according to some notion of what it ought to be.

Music

The word 'Romanticism', at first applied mainly to literature and painting, was taken up by late 19th-century musicians to describe the shifts in musical style that took place in the early years of that century. In their music, Romantic composers aimed for greater freedom of form, emotional intensity and expression of personal feeling. Often a musician was inspired by paintings or landscapes

— LINES FROM 'THE CLOUD' —
BY SHELLEY

'I bring fresh showers for the thirsting flowers,
From the seas and the streams;
I bear light shade for the leaves when laid
In their noonday dreams.
From my wings are shaken the dews that waken
The sweet buds every one,
When rocked to rest on their mother's breast,
As she dances about the Sun.
I wield the flail of the lashing hail,
And whiten the green plains under,
And then again I dissolve it in rain,
And laugh as I pass in thunder.'

. . .

'I bind the Sun's throne with a burning zone,
And the Moon's with a girdle of pearl;
The volcanoes are dim, and the stars reel and swim,
When the whirlwinds my banner unfurl.
From cape to cape, with a bridge-like shape,
Over a torrent sea,
Sunbeam-proof, I hang like a roof —
The mountains its columns be!
The triumphal arch, through which I march
With hurricane, fire, and snow,
When the Powers of the air, are chained to my chair,
Is the million-coloured bow;
The sphere-fire above its soft colours wove,
While the moist Earth was laughing below.'

_____

J.M.W. Turner (1775-1851)
Rain, Steam and Speed (1844)
Notwithstanding the general Romantic dislike of mechanization
and industrialization, Turner has in this painting captured the
romance of an early railway train as it pushes across a bridge
through swirling rain. Some contemporary viewers thought that
the 'Speed' in the title referred to the hare running before the
locomotive.

he had seen, or a book or poem he had read, or by friendship and discussion with fellow artists in the fields of painting or literature. Like Romantic writers and artists, composers were also fascinated by fantasy and the supernatural, exotic lands and dream landscapes, legends and fairy tales. In the opera *Der Freischütz* ('The Magic Marksman' 1821) by Karl Weber (1786-1826), there are many of these elements. This was the first important German Romantic opera, based on a story from folklore that had close parallels to Goethe's *Faust* (see box), in which a man sells his soul to the devil in return for favors on Earth. As Romantic composers strived for greater expression through their music, harmonies became more complex and orchestration more colorful. Some of the most spectacular musical canvases of the Romantic age include the orchestral works of Hector Berlioz (1803-69) and the operas of Richard Wagner (1813-83).

The early spirit of the dawning Romantic Age in music was epitomized by the works and person of Ludwig van Beethoven (1770-1827). In his music, he pushed the forms and sounds of the Classical period to their limits in his search for a new vocabulary and expressiveness in music. His *Eroica* Symphony (No.3 1803), for example, is full of the energy, wildness and Romantic passion which he saw sweeping across Europe. Beethoven dedicated this symphony to Napoleon Bonaparte, as a tribute to the hero of liberated, revolutionary France (see page 24 and illustration opposite). However, when Napoleon declared himself Emperor in 1804, Beethoven tore off the title page on which the dedication was written and wrote instead: 'Heroic Symphony, composed to celebrate the memory of a great man'. Beethoven's hatred of tyranny and celebration of the ideals of the French Revolution were also apparent in his choice of subject for his only opera, *Fidelio* (1805). The opera is set in a prison, and concerns the rescue of one of the prisoners by his faithful and heroic wife. It

— THE IMPACT OF ROMANTIC — WRITERS UPON PAINTING AND MUSIC

It has often been the case through the ages that literature has inspired painters and musicians: witness the number of paintings and amount of incidental illustrating scenes based on the works of Shakespeare. The same was true of the Romantic writers. The German playwright Johann Wolfgang von Goethe (1749-1832), considered by many to be one of the greatest Romantic writers, inspired many composers with his Faust (1808, 1832). This poetic drama in two parts reworked the story of the man whose intellectual cravings lead him to sell his soul to the devil. Composers inspired by the Faust story included the Hungarian Franz Liszt (1811-86), who wrote a symphony based on the story, and the Frenchmen Hector Berlioz and Charles Gounod (1818-93) who both wrote dramatic settings. Gounod also composed settings of poetry by Wordsworth, Shelley and Byron, among others.

Byron was a major source of inspiration for many musicians and artists. The French painter Delacroix claimed that Byron 'inflamed his imagination' and inspired him to paint Marino Faliero (1825-6) and The Death of Sardanapalus (1827), taken from scenes in two of Byron's plays. On 14 May 1824, the very day that news of Byron's death in Greece reached London, Delacroix wrote in his diary that 'Byron gives me an insatiable longing to create'. The Italian composer Guiseppe Verdi (1813-1901), an ardent Italian nationalist, admired Byron's vision for the liberty of Greece and was influenced by his work in general. Verdi adapted Byron's The Two Foscari into an opera in 1843, and later The Corsair (1848).

———————

Jacques-Louis David (1748-1825)
Napoleon Crossing the Alps **(1800)**
David's painting is an idealized image of Napoleon on a rearing horse against a wild Romantic landscape. Initially the Romantics saw in Napoleon a leader who would continue the spirit of the French Revolution and bring greater liberty and democracy to the French and other European peoples. But in 1804, when Napoleon made himself Emperor of France, these hopes were finally dashed.

deals with issues of freedom and justice, and reaches a climax as all the prisoners are released from the prison.

Like many of the Romantic poets, Beethoven found inspiration for his work in Nature. He often composed outdoors, while taking long walks. He described this process in the following words:

> 'You will ask me whence I take my ideas? That I cannot say with any degree of certainty; they come to me uninvited, directly or indirectly. I could almost grasp them in my hands, out in Nature's open, in the woods, during my promenades, in the silence of the night, at the earliest dawn. They are roused by moods which in the poet's case are transmuted into words, and in mine into tones, that sound, roar and storm until at last they take shape for me as notes.'

Romantic song

Not all Romantic music was on a large scale. There was a flowering of song (known by the German word for 'song': *lied*, plural *lieder*) during the Romantic period, especially in Germany. Franz Schubert (1797-1828), an Austrian by birth, composed more than 600 songs in his short life, displaying in them a range of mood, emotion and drama unknown before his time. Among his best known are *Erlkönig* ('The Erl-king' 1815), composed when he was only 18 to words by Goethe. This song dramatically relates a tale of dark mischief done by the Erl-king, who tries to seduce a boy out of the arms of his father as the two ride through the forest at night. He fails, but the icy grasp of the Erl-king has touched the boy, and when they reach home he is dead. In performance piano and voice combine to draw out the Romantic terror of the story. No longer does the piano merely play a supporting role, providing harmony for the voice. Instead it takes an integral part in the drama of the song, with pounding chords depicting the frantic galloping of the horse. Schubert, and another notable *lied* composer, Robert Schumann (1810-56), also wrote sequences of songs, called song cycles, which are linked together to relate a story. An example is Schubert's desolate song cycle known as *Winterreise* ('Winter Journey' 1827), which was written at a time when Schubert was coming to terms with illness and his own imminent death. Schumann's song-cycles include *Frauenliebe und Leben* ('A Woman's Love and Life' 1840) and *Dichterliebe* ('A Poet's Love' 1840).

Musical pictures

The 19th century saw the development of 'program music' – instrumental music that aimed to tell a story or paint a musical picture without the use of words. The interest in the concept of program music arose through closer links between music, literature and painting. For example, Beethoven's *Pastoral* Symphony

(No.6 1808) aimed to evoke in the mind of the listener a Romantic landscape. In the symphony there are such musical depictions as a peasants' merry-making, birdcalls and a storm, although Beethoven claimed that his symphony was 'more of an expression of feeling than a painting'. The French composer Hector Berlioz was more direct in his *Symphonie Fantastique* ('Fantastic Symphony' 1830), supplying program notes to an extended five-movement symphony (instead of the usual four movements) subtitled 'Episodes in the Life of an Artist'. The movements depict a young musician dreaming of his passion for his beloved; whirling dancers at a ball; a walk in fields including shepherds' pipes; a sunset and distant thunder; a march to the scaffold – the artist dreams that in a fit of jealousy he has murdered his beloved – at the end of which we hear the rapid downward slide of the guillotine; and finally a nightmare of a witches' sabbath in which funeral bells and chants for the dead are played.

Other examples of music which aimed to evoke a landscape or a narrative include Felix Mendelssohn's (1809-47) sea-picture *The Hebrides* (1832), also known as *Fingal's Cave* (a cavern associated with romantic legends in Staffa, one of the inner Hebrides, and a place also visited by Keats). In the late Romantic period music began to be used as an expression of nationalism and patriotic fervor, for example in the music of composers such as the Russian, Mikhail Glinka (1804-57), who attempted to portray a picture of their country in music.

Theatre

The Romantic Age did not produce a significant number of new plays. Many writers of the time tried their hand at the stage, but their efforts were more dramatic poems than dramas, and little of what they wrote had notable success at the time or later. Among these attempts were Shelley's *The Cenci* (1819) and *Prometheus Unbound* and Byron's *Manfred* (1817), which was set against the Alpine backdrop so beloved of him and the Shelleys. *Manfred* featured a satiated, rebellious hero and was patently autobiographical. However, several of Byron's plays such as *Marino*

– THE PERFORMER AS HERO –

The Romantic period saw the rise of the virtuosi — performers capable of dazzling technique and great expressiveness. These performers epitomized the Romantic concept of the artist as hero. At the same time, improvements in the design and construction of instruments such as the piano allowed composers and performers to exploit a greater range and richness of sound. Beethoven was a pianist of exceptional virtuosity, who pushed the instrument of his time to the limits. But the most spectacular virtuoso pianist was the Hungarian Franz Liszt. He wrote many pieces for the piano, including arrangements of orchestral works such as Berlioz's Symphonie Fantastique *(see main text), and his solo recitals soon became the stuff of legend. Liszt was himself inspired by another virtuoso, the Italian violinist Niccolò Paganini (1782-1840). Paganini's renowned technique and artistry on his instrument dazzled all those who heard him and led some to question whether he had made some sinister Faustian pact with the devil. Another notable virtuoso pianist and composer was the Polish Fryderyk Chopin (1810-49), whose delicate playing was celebrated in the salons of Paris.*

Faliero (1821), a political drama set in medieval Venice, were produced on the stage during the 1820s. *Marino Faliero* also inspired the great Italian opera composer Gaetano Donizetti (1797-1848) to compose an opera of the same name.

Most new plays were thin sentimental comedies or farces. Tragedies by the German writers Johann Wolfgang von Goethe (see box page 68) and Johann von Schiller (1759-1805) were translated for the English stage, with Wordsworth dismissing them as 'sickly and stupid German tragedies' (see box). The best writers of the time were not dramatists, and this may be why Scott's novels were often dramatized soon after publication.

Nonetheless the Romantic period was an age of famous actors and actresses, including Edmund Kean (1787-1833), Philip Kemble (1775-1854) and his sister Sarah Siddons (1755-1831), and Charles Macready (1793-1873). The period also produced some thought-provoking and highly readable dramatic criticism. Mrs Siddons's Lady Macbeth was admired as particularly impressive; Hazlitt considered Kemble 'too deliberate and formal' as Hamlet; and witnessing the dynamic and passionate Kean was, according to Coleridge, 'like reading Shakespeare by flashes of lightning'. Thomas De Quincey analyzed in detail the dramatic effect of the knocking at the gate which follows the murder of Duncan in *Macbeth*; Lamb felt that the 18th-century adapter Nahum Tate (1652-1715) had done well to make *King Lear* stageable by changing the ending into a happy one; and he and Hazlitt both mused upon the characters of Shakespeare as objects of intellectual meditation, fitter for study than the stage. However, no character drew contemporary interest more than Hamlet, whose intelligence, wit, irresolution, world-weariness, and combination of introspection and passionate action embodied what many Romantics felt about themselves.

— STURM UND DRANG—

Sturm und Drang – *'Storm and Stress'—was a German pre-Romantic movement which led to the kind of theatre to which Wordsworth objected so strongly (see main text). The phrase comes from a play by Friedrich Klinger (1752-1831), a protegé of Goethe. Typical Sturm und Drang dramas stressed the importance of the individual and ignored convention in art and other respects. They also involved idealism, patriotism and worship of the power of genius. The following is a contemporary report of a performance of a play in the Sturm und Drang style by Schiller called* The Robbers *(1781), which caused a sensation:*

'The theatre was like a madhouse: rolling eyeballs, clenched fists, stamping feet, hoarse cries in the auditorium! Complete strangers fell sobbing into each other's arms, women staggered almost fainting to the door. It was a general state of dissolution, like a chaos from whose mists a new creation is breaking forth.'

———————————

6. THE GOTHIC AND SUPERNATURAL

'Gothic', originally referring to the Germanic tribe of Goths who helped to overwhelm the western Roman Empire in the fifth century AD, came to define a style of medieval church and castle architecture that incorporated high, soaring vaulted roofs, flying buttresses, and narrow pointed arches and windows. By the 18th century the word had come to signify the mysteries that accompanied the dim medieval world from which the Gothic sprang.

Gothic literature appealed to the same sentiments as those excited by the sublime in art (see page 61), dealing as it did with the passionate, mysterious, horrific and supernatural. It was especially popular in Britain between the 1760s and 1820s. Stories were often set in the medieval past, or in foreign countries, where castles, convents and dark, labyrinthine passages became the scenes for both physical and mental imprisonment – or worse, the perpetration of physical and moral outrages. Characteristic backdrops to these 'horrid' tales were picturesque ruins (haunted places according to superstition) full of sinister possibilities involving ghosts, witches, sorcerers, wizards, shape-changing dwarfs, and wonderful and terrible natural effects.

Horace Walpole's novel *The Castle of Otranto* (1764) is generally considered to be the earliest example of the Gothic genre. In writing it, Walpole was reacting to the inflexible rationality of his day. In a letter of 9 March 1765 he wrote of the importance of his irrational subconscious in the genesis of the story:

'I waked one morning in the beginning of last June from a dream, of which all I could recover was, that I thought myself in an ancient castle (a very natural dream for a head filled like mine with Gothic story) and that on the uppermost banister of a great staircase I saw a gigantic hand in armour. In the evening I sat down and began to write, without knowing in the least what I intended to say or relate.'

His story is sub-titled 'a Gothic story' mainly on account of its medieval setting. In fact, Walpole initially claimed that the book was a translation from an Italian original. It is also Gothic in its use of irrational incident and the surreal (see Glossary of Terms): the plot includes a moving portrait that sighs, an enormous helmet that falls out of the sky and crushes somebody to death, a ghost that grows too large for a castle and tears it down, and a statue that bleeds and walks.

The Castle of Otranto was the first in a flourishing genre of Gothic novels. It was followed by the accomplished works of Ann Radcliffe who, with titles such as The Mysteries of Udolpho and The Italian (1797), became one of the most celebrated writers of Gothic literature. Other writers who turned their hands to the Gothic included William Godwin (see box page 16) with Caleb Williams (1794), M.G. Lewis (1775-1818) with his phenomenally successful novel The Monk (1796), William Beckford (1760-1844) with Vathek (1786) – which Byron called his Bible – and Mary Shelley with Frankenstein (see page 78). It has been well said that Gothic novels were calculated to keep the reader awake at night. The following extract from The Mysteries of Udolpho gives a flavor of the genre:

> 'The image of her aunt murdered – murdered, perhaps, by the hand of Montoni, rose to her mind; she trembled, gasped for breath – repented that she had dared to venture hither, and checked her steps. But, after she had paused for a few minutes, the consciousness of her duty returned, and she went on. Still all was silent. At length a track of blood, upon a stair, caught her eye; and instantly she perceived, that the wall and several other steps were stained. She paused, again struggled to support herself, and the lamp almost fell from her trembling hand. Still no sound was heard, no living being seemed to inhabit the turret; a thousand times she wished herself again in her chamber; dreaded to enquire farther – dreaded to encounter some horrible spectacle...'

Romantic excess

Some writers of the period satirized the prevailing philosophies of Romantic fashion. Thomas Love Peacock poked fun at the excesses of the Gothic novel in Headlong Hall (1816) and Nightmare Abbey (1818). In fact, most of the leading writers of the day, including Coleridge and Shelley, were caricatured and satirized in the latter work. Jane Austen, while not unappreciative of the main drive of Romanticism, remained aware of where Romantic excess could lead. In Northanger Abbey her heroine, Catherine Morland, is introduced to the delights of Gothic novels by her new-found friend Isabella Thorpe. The two read The Mysteries of Udolpho, and Isabella promises Catherine the prospect of many more similar tales to delight her sense of terror:

> '"Dear creature!... when you have finished Udolpho, we will read the Italian together; and I have made a list of ten or twelve more of the same kind for you."

"Have you indeed! How glad I am! –
What are they all?"

"I will read you their names directly;
here they are, in my pocket-book.
Castle of Wolfenbach, Clermont,
Mysterious Warnings, Necromancer of
the Black Forest, Midnight Bell,
Orphan of the Rhine, and Horrid
Mysteries. Those will last us some
time."

"Yes pretty well; but are they all
horrid, are you sure they are all
horrid?"'

Catherine is eventually shaken out of
her Gothic fantasies with a dawning
realization that '...charming as were all of
Mrs Radcliffe's works, and charming even
as were the works of all her imitators, it
was not in them perhaps that human
nature, at least in the midland counties
of England, was to be looked for.'
Likewise in *Sense and Sensibility* (1811)
Austen points out the dangers of
abandoning sense in favor of the
excessively Romantic and self-centered
sensibility (see box) that nearly kills
Marianne. Indeed, Jane Austen's world
was an essentially sensible and
unromantic place, and this may explain
why at the time her novels did not sell
well, only two of them reaching a second
edition in her lifetime. Her writing was too
realistic, too subtle and not sensational
enough for the taste of most novel readers of the Romantic Age.
However, her reputation rose steadily during the Victorian period
and has never since waned.

— SENSIBILITY—

*Sensibility is a term used to denote the ability to respond
with feeling and sympathy, even empathy, to a circumstance,
book or other artistic form, especially in relation to aspects
of beauty or to the plight of others. The term became popular in the late 18th century, and the cult of sensibility arose
in reaction to some of the more insensitive aspects of 18th-
century life, such as the hedonistic pleasure-seeking of the
moneyed classes in the towns, and the boorish ignorance of
country gentry such as Squire Western in Henry Fielding's*
Tom Jones *(1749). In literary terms, the Age of Sensibility
came to define a period from about 1744 (the death of
Pope) until somewhere around the end of the 18th century.
In general, this period sees a reaction against the cynicism
of the Restoration and the writings of such as Thomas Hobbes
(1588-1679), and the beginnings of the movement toward
Romanticism and the elevation of feeling above neo-
Classical intellectualism and 'correctness'. Examples of rele-
vant works are Gray's 'Elegy' (1751), Sterne's* A
Sentimental Journey Through France and Italy
(1767), Goldsmith's The Deserted Village *and William
Cowper's (1731-1800)* The Task *(1785). European
examples include Goethe's* The Sorrows of Young
Werther *(1774) and the novels of Rousseau. In Radcliffe's*
The Mysteries of Udolpho *the heroine, after many terri-
fying adventures, including escape from the clutches of a
wicked guardian, marries a man who is a model of sensibility. It was considered that to react with sensibility was
proof of moral virtue in an individual; but this sometimes
descended into sentimentality, Sheridan satirizing hypocritical sentiment in his play* The School for Scandal *(1777).*

Coleridge and the Gothic imagination

After its early development in the novel, the Gothic began to extend
into other kinds of literature. Coleridge's *The Rime of the Ancient
Mariner* contains many elements of Gothic horror: the ice-scapes of
the polar regions, the dead men getting to their feet to sail the
boat, the Ancient Mariner biting his arm to draw blood so that his
throat is moist enough to cry "A sail! A sail!" as the specter ship

comes toward his boat. The poem includes the classic Gothic elements of hallucination, nightmare and death, and a Romantic sole survivor, half-crazed by his experiences, who tries to make sense of it all. Coleridge believed that through the exercise of the imagination we reach understandings denied to us if we exercise only on a strictly logical plane.

Another poem that, according to Coleridge, was the result of the transcendence of imagination over the rational mind was 'Kubla Khan'. There is something of a mystery, probably encouraged by Coleridge himself, surrounding the manner in which this poem came to be written. Coleridge was staying at a secluded farmhouse high up on the edge of Exmoor. He was reading Samuel Purchas's *Pilgrimage*, an early 17th-century travel book about voyages to various places, including the far-off land of the Mughal emperor Kubla Khan. Having taken an 'anodyne' (almost certainly laudanum, an opium-based drug) as a pain-killer, Coleridge fell asleep. While asleep, his dreams seem to have included fantastic Gothic elements such as huge caverns, deep chasms, a savage enchanted place, a wailing woman and a demon lover. When Coleridge awoke he had, he claimed, an entire 300-word poem in his mind. He began to write it down, but after committing only 50 or so lines to paper he was interrupted 'by a person on business from Porlock'. When he returned to his desk some time later he could remember little of the rest, and so the poem remained 'A fragment' (Coleridge's sub-title). Considerable doubt has been cast upon this version of events, which Coleridge appended as a note to the poem when Byron finally persuaded him to publish it in 1816.

Frankenstein and after

A transformation involving encounters with the frightening, the uncanny and the semi-human, as seen in *The Rime of the Ancient Mariner,* was very much a part of the Gothic tradition. These elements are present in Coleridge's 'Christabel' (1816), Keats's 'Lamia' (1820) and in Mary Shelley's *Frankenstein*, now the most famous Gothic novel of the period. In 1816, the Shelleys and a friend of Byron's called Dr Polidori were staying with Byron at Villa Diodati, a large house that he had rented on the shores of Lake Geneva in Switzerland. Topics of conversation there included the source of life, contemporary theories of anthropology, and the possible effects of

— LINES FROM 'KUBLA KHAN' —

'In Xanadu did Kubla Khan
A stately pleasure-dome decree:
Where Alph, the sacred river, ran
Through caverns measureless to man
Down to a sunless sea.
So twice five miles of fertile ground
With walls and towers were girdled round:
And there were gardens bright with sinuous rills,
Where blossomed many an incense-bearing tree;
And here were forests ancient as the hills,
Enfolding sunny spots of greenery...'

Caspar David Friedrich (1774-1840)
The Polar Sea **(1824)**

Ice-scapes were one of the kinds of wild places very popular
with the Romantics. For example, the opening and closing
scenes of Mary Shelley's *Frankenstein* take place in and
around a ship frozen in the Arctic wastes, and Coleridge's
Ancient Mariner finds himself at the South Pole, with ice
'mast high... all around'.

electricity in stimulating the human body and life itself. One night, Mary had a hideous dream, inspired by a passage in the writings of the physician and poet Erasmus Darwin (1731-1802; grandfather of Charles Darwin), in which he talks of experimenting with the artificial creation of life. Mary may also have known of the experiments of the time in the making of automata by French scientists and others. Some time after this dream, Byron proposed a ghost story competition in which he, Percy Shelley and Mary should all take part. Only Mary finished her story – *Frankenstein*. It is interesting to note – long before the founder of psychoanalysis Sigmund Freud (1865-1939) wrote of the significance of dreams – that Mary Shelley and Coleridge both claimed the origin of their stories to be dreams. Throughout the book, Mary Shelley uses a literary version of Burke's 'power of obscurity' (see page 61) by avoiding any exact descriptions of horror. Instead she draws the reader's attention to the reactions of the narrator. This prevents the objects of horror from descending into the mundane or laughable, and allows the reader to bring the imagination to work on what the narrator is seeing.

Other writing with Gothic elements includes De Quincey's *Confessions of an English Opium Eater* (1821). His examination of the way the mind works had considerable influence upon the stories of Edgar Allan Poe (1808-49), among others, and possibly the Brontës in their imaginative use of the Gothic. Later novels that incorporate what has been called 'the psychological Gothic' include James Hogg's (1770-1835) *Memoirs and Confessions of a Justified Sinner* (1824), in which the Gothic takes the form of the extreme religious mania of the protagonist, who is possessed by the devil; Emily Brontë's *Wuthering Heights* (1847); Charlotte Brontë's *Jane Eyre* (1847); and Dickens's *Great Expectations* (1861). The genre of the Gothic was continued in the 20th century

— JOURNAL-LETTER FROM — SHELLEY TO THOMAS LOVE PEACOCK

Shelley was awed by the sublime and Romantic grandeur of the Alps. In this letter to Thomas Love Peacock he described Mont Blanc, which towers above the valley of Chamonix in France. Compare this prose account of his experiences with the extract from the poem 'Mont Blanc' on page 62:

'*22 August 1816 From Servox, three leagues remain to Chamonix. Mont Blanc was before us. The Alps with their innumerable glaciers on high, all around, closing in the complicated windings of the single vale; forests inexpressibly beautiful, but majestic in their beauty; interwoven beech and pine and oak overshadowed our road, or receded whilst lawns of such verdure as I have never seen before occupied these openings, and, extending gradually, becoming darker into their recesses.*

Mont Blanc was before us but was covered with cloud, and its base furrowed with dreadful gaps was seen alone. Pinnacles of snow, intolerably bright, part of the chain connected with Mont Blanc, shone through the clouds at intervals on high. I never knew, I never imagined what mountains were before. The immensity of the aerial summits excited, when they suddenly burst upon the sight, a sentiment of ecstatic wonder not unallied to madness. And remember this was all one scene. It all pressed home to our regard and to our imagination. Though it embraced a great number of miles, the snowy pyramids which shot into the bright blue sky seemed to overhang our path; the ravine, clothed with gigantic pines and black with its depth below (so deep that the very roaring of the untameable Arve which rolled through it could not be heard above), was close to our very footsteps. All was as much our own as if we had been the creators of such impressions in the minds of others, as now occupied our own. Nature was the poet whose harmony held our spirits more breathless than that of the divinest.'

_____

by authors such as William Faulkner (1897-1962), Isak Dinesen (1885-1962), Mervyn Peake (1911-68) and Angela Carter (1940-92).

Romantic fascination with the medieval

Seen by the Augustan writers as a time of darkness and superstition, the medieval period attracted the Romantics for various reasons. The perception of the Middle Ages as a time of courtly love and nobility, when feudal ties meant that people knew their place in society, compared favorably to the rapidly changing society brought about by the changes of the Industrial Revolution. There was also an element of escapism, of the possibilities of the dim and distant past, which excited the Romantic imagination. During his apprenticeship to James Basire (see box page 60), Blake spent long hours sketching the figures of the tombs in Westminster Abbey: the flowing lines of the Gothic figures and the soaring Gothic architecture above him deeply affected both his artistic and poetic style. The abbey also generated in him an imaginative vision of English history which he felt had been lost during the rationalism of the 18th century. In a similar way Gothic architecture was to inspire the French Romantic author Victor Hugo (1802-85) in *Notre Dame de Paris* (1831, commonly known as *The Hunchback of Notre Dame*).

Attempts to recreate the 'medieval' in architecture were seen at Strawberry Hill (see page 58), at Fonthill Abbey in Wiltshire (home of William Beckford, see page 74), and in the 'Gothicized' exteriors of places such as Belvoir Castle in Leicestershire and Windsor

— WORDSWORTH EXPERIENCES—
THE GOTHIC IN NATURE

In the following extract from The Prelude, *Wordsworth describes how, as a child, he rowed out into a lake. As he rowed, a mountain seemed to rear its head up above the horizon and the harder he rowed, the more it seemed to pursue him. After returning the boat he explains how a kind of Gothic horror brooded in his mind for days afterwards, the effect of a seemingly deliberate and alarming action by a living Nature. What Wordsworth actually experienced was parallax, a phenomenon whereby as one moves away from an object it seems to grow larger as more of it appears behind a smaller object in front of it:*

> '...I fixed my view
> Upon the summit of a craggy ridge,
> The horizon's utmost boundary; far above
> Was nothing but the stars and the grey sky.
> She was an elfin pinnace; lustily
> I dipped my oars into the silent lake
> And, as I rose upon the stroke, my boat
> Went heaving through the water like a swan,
> When, from behind that craggy steep till then
> The horizon's bound, a huge peak, black and huge,
> As if with voluntary power instinct
> Upreared its head. I struck and struck again
> And growing still in stature the grim shape
> Towered up between me and the stars, and still,
> With measured motion like a living thing,
> Strode after me. With trembling oars I turned,
> And through the silent water stole my way
> Back to the covert of the willow tree;
> There in her mooring place I left my bark,
> And through the meadow homeward went, in grave
> And serious mood; and after I had seen
> That spectacle, for many days my brain
> Worked with a dim and undetermined sense
> Of unknown modes of being; o'er my thoughts
> There hung a darkness, call it solitude
> Or blank desertion. No familiar shapes
> Remained, no pleasant images of tress,
> Of sea or sky, no colours of green fields;
> But huge and mighty forms that do not live,
> Like living men moved slowly through the mind
> By day, and were a trouble to my dreams.'

Castle. However, this type of recreation also found its way into literature. The pseudo-medieval verses of Thomas Chatterton (see page 13) made use of 'medievalized' spellings, and particularly influenced Keats. In 'The Eve of St Mark' (1819), Keats followed Chatterton in writing part of the poem in mock medieval verse:

> ' "Als writith he of swevenis,
> Men han beforne they wake in bliss,
> Whanne that hir friends thinke hem bound
> In crimped shroude farre under ground;
> And how a litling child mote be
> A saint er its nativitie,
> Gif that the modre (God her blesse!)
> Kepen in solitarinesse,
> And kissen devoute the holy croce.'

Keats's fascination with the medieval led him to give several of his poems a medieval flavor and setting, for example 'La Belle Dame sans Merci' (1820) and 'The Eve of St Agnes', from which this extract is taken:

> 'A casement high and triple-arch'd there was.
> All garlanded with carven imag'ries
> Of fruits, and flowers, and bunches of knot-grass,
> And diamonded with panes of quaint device,
> Innumerable of stains and splendid dyes,
> As are the tiger-moth's deep-damask wings;
> And in the midst, 'mong thousand heraldries,
> And twilight saints, and dim emblazonings,
> A shielded scutcheon blush'd with blood of queens and kings.'

Keats gives a graphic description here of a typically Gothic window, 'triple-arch'd', surrounded by lavish stone ornamentation, and set with stained glass, and instantly recognizable in Victorian 'Gothic' churches throughout Britain.

POSTSCRIPT
Post-Romanticism and neo-Romanticism

At the beginning of the book it was noted that nobody saw the Romantic Age as drawing to a precise close in 1840. It can be argued that the Post-Romantic era began in the 1830s and that all ages since, whether defined as Victorian, Modern or post-Modern, contain elements of Romanticism, and that we are all, in some senses, post-Romantics. There is a direct line from Coleridge to Jack Kerouac (1922-69) and the Beat Movement of the 1950s, and to the hippies of the 1960s, who showed many traits of Romantic feeling such as idealism, nature-worship, fascination with oriental cultures, political or social rebellion and opposition to established institutions. 'Just do your own thing', a mantra of the hippies, was a Romantic exhortation to be an individual and not to feel forced by society into doing what you felt was inappropriate. The music group 'The Incredible String Band' wrote of Byronic flashing eyes and floating hair. And those who attend the pop music festivals outdoors also are playing with the idea of Romanticism. As one critic has put it: 'We are still living in the comet's tail of the early 19th century.'

Post-Modern thinkers will consider that such simplistic passion as Keats's 'Beauty is truth, truth beauty, – that is all/ Ye know on earth, and all ye need to know' ('Ode on a Grecian Urn') and the neo-Romantic affirmation by the Beatles that 'All you need is love' must be questioned. Yet it is worth bearing in mind the words of one senior Liberal politician when asked whether he considered that Margaret Thatcher, the Conservative Prime Minister of the 1980s, ever thought about nuclear war. 'Oh yes', he replied, 'I'm sure that she thinks about it; but I doubt that she ever imagines about it.' Perhaps, in the final analysis, imagination – in every context of human endeavor – is the key to Romanticism.

— CARPE DIEM (II) —

These two extracts are both modern pieces of writing in which the Romantic spirit of carpe diem, *'seize the day", is evident. (Compare them with the extract from Shelley in the box on page 11.) The first is 'The Bright Field' (1975) by the Welsh poet R. S. Thomas (1913-2000). The second is an extract from the novel* The Color Purple *(1983) by the American writer Alice Walker (b.1944):*

*'I have seen the sun break through
To illuminate a small field
For a while, and gone my way
And forgotten it. But that was the pearl
Of great price, the one field that had
The treasure in it. I realise now
That I must give all that I have
To possess it. Life is not hurrying*

*On to a receding future, not hankering after
An imagined past. It is the turning
Aside like Moses to the miracle
Of the lit bush, to a brightness
That seemed as transitory as your youth
Once, but is the eternity that awaits you.'*

'I think it pisses God off if you walk by the color purple in a field somewhere and you don't notice it.'

_____

TIMELINE

Science, technology and other arts	Literature	History
	1754 Rousseau *Discourse*	
	1755 Johnson *Dictionary*	**1756** Beginning of Seven
	1757 Burke *A Philosophical*	Years' War (to 1763)
	Enquiry into the Origin of	
	our Ideas of the Sublime	
	and the Beautiful	**1760** George II dies;
		succeeded by George III
	1761 Rousseau *La Nouvelle*	
	Héloïse	
	1762 Rousseau *The Social*	**1763** French cede overseas
	Contract; *Émile, ou*	territory to British
	l'Education	Proclamation to prevent
		westwards expansion of
		North American colonies
1764 Hargreaves invents	**1764** Walpole *Castle of*	**1764** Sugar Act in
spinning jenny	*Otranto*	American colonies
	1765 Bishop Percy *Reliques*	**1765** Stamp Act in
	of Ancient English Poetry	American colonies
	1767 Sterne *A Sentimental*	
1768 Royal Academy of Arts	*Journey Through France and*	
founded in London	*Italy*	**1774** First Continental
1769 Arkwright invents water		Congress in American
frame	**1770** Goldsmith *The*	colonies
1775 Watt develops steam	*Deserted Village*	**1775** American
engine	Death of Chatterton	Revolutionary War (to 1781)
1779 Crompton develops	**1775** Sheridan *The Rivals*	**1776** American Declaration
spinning mule	**1777** Sheridan *The School*	of Independence (4 July)
1780 American Academy of	*for Scandal*	**1780** Gordon riots (anti-
Sciences founded in Boston		Roman Catholic) in London
1781 Hershel discovers the	**1782** Blake *Poetical*	**1783** Britain recognizes
planet Uranus	*Sketches*	American independence
1782 Haydn *Six Quartets*	Rousseau *Confessions* (to	**1784** Wesley's Deed of
(Op. 33)	1789)	Declaration, the charter of
Montgolfier brothers in	**1785** Cowper *The Task*	Wesleyan Methodism
France construct air balloon	**1786** Beckford *Vathek*	**1787** Founding of Society
1784 Reynolds *Portrait of*	Burns *Poems, Chiefly in the*	for the Abolition of the
Mrs Siddons as the Tragic	*Scottish Dialect*	Slave Trade
Muse	Gilpin *Tour of the Lakes*	**1788** George III's first attack
1787 Mozart *Eine Kleine*		of mental illness
Nachtmusik and *Don*	**1788** Blake *Natural Religion*	**1789** Washington first
Giovanni	**1789** Blake *Songs of*	President of the United
1789 First steam-powered	*Innocence*	States
spinning loom speeds up		French Revolution begins
textile production		Bentham *Introduction to*
		the Principles of Morals
		and Legislation

1790 Lavoisier *Table of Thirty-One Chemical Elements*
Wright of Derby *An Italian Landscape with Mountains and a River*

1791 Mozart *The Magic Flute*

1793 Haydn *'London'* symphonies
David *The Death of Marat*

1794 Blake *The Ancient of Days*
First telegraph established in France (Paris to Lille)

1795 Haydn *The Military* (No. 100) and *The Clock* (No. 101) symphonies
Paris Conservatoire de Musique founded
1797 Haydn *Emperor* Quartet (Op. 76)
1799 Haydn *The Creation*
Turner *Buttermere Lake: A Shower*
1800 David *Napoleon Crossing the Alps*
Volta invents electric battery

1803 Beethoven *Eroica* Symphony (No.3)
1804 Turner *The Passage of the St Gothard*
1805 Beethoven *Fidelio*

1790 Blake *The Marriage of Heaven and Hell*
Burke *Reflections on the Revolution in France*
Wollstonecraft *A Vindication of the Rights of Men*
1791 Blake *The French Revolution*
Paine *The Rights of Man* Pt 1
1792 Gilpin *Three Essays on Picturesque Beauty*
Paine *The Rights of Man* Pt 2
Wollstonecraft *Vindication of the Rights of Women*
1793 Blake *America: A Prophecy, Visions of the Daughters of Albion*
Godwin *Enquiry concerning Political Justice*
Wordsworth 'An Evening Walk', *Descriptive Sketches*
1794 Blake *Songs of Innocence and of Experience, The First Book of Urizen*
Godwin *Caleb Williams*
Paine *The Age of Reason*
Radcliffe *Mysteries of Udolpho*

1795 Blake *The Song of Los*
Wordsworth meets Coleridge
1796 Coleridge *Poems on Various Subjects*
Lewis *The Monk*
1797 Radcliffe *The Italian*
1798 Wordsworth and Coleridge *Lyrical Ballads*
1799 Southey *Poems*

1800 Blake *Job and his Daughters*
Lyrical Ballads (2nd ed.)

1802 Scott *The Minstrelsy of the Scottish Border* (to 1803)

1804 Blake *Jerusalem*
1805 Scott *The Lay of the Last Minstrel*
Wordsworth *Elegiac Stanzas*

1790 Louis XVI agrees to new constitution in France

1791 Wilberforce's motion for abolition of the slave trade defeated in Parliament
1792 French Republic is declared
September Massacres in Paris

1793 Execution of Louis XVI
Reign of Terror in France
Gagging Acts and suspension of Habeas Corpus in Britain

1794 Robespierre guillotined
Slavery abolished in French colonies

1795 Speenhamland Act for poor relief in Britain

1798 France invades Switzerland
Malthus *Essay on the Principle of Population*
1799 Napoleon becomes First Consul
1801 Act of Union joins Ireland politically to England
1802 Peace of Amiens between Britain and France
1803 Renewal of hostilities between Britain and France
1804 Napoleon crowns himself Emperor of France
1805 Battle of Trafalgar

Science, technology and other arts	Literature	History
1806 Ingres *Napoleon*	**1807** Wordsworth *Poems in Two Volumes*	**1807** Abolition of slave trade in British Empire
1808 Beethoven *Pastoral Symphony* (No. 6)	**1808** Goethe *Faust* Pt 1	**1808** Peninsular War in Spain
1809 Friedrich *Abbey in an Oak Forest*	Scott *Marmion*	
1810 Friedrich *Cloister Graveyard in the Snow*	**1810** Scott *The Lady of the Lake*	
	1811 Austen *Sense and Sensibility*	**1811** George III permanently insane; Prince of Wales becomes Regent
	Shelley *The Necessity of Atheism*	
1812 David *Napoleon in his Study*	**1812** Byron *Childe Harold* Cantos 1 and 2	**1812** Failure of French invasion of Russia
Elgin marbles brought to Britain from Greece	**1813** Byron *The Giaour, The Bride of Abydos*	**1813** Austria and Prussia declare war on France
Davy *Elements of Chemical Philosophy*	Shelley *Queen Mab*	Wellington victorious in Peninsular War
1814 Beethoven *Fidelio*	**1814** Byron *The Corsair, Lara*	**1814** Napoleon abdicates and is exiled to Elba
Goya *The Third of May, 1808*	Scott *Waverley*	
	Wordsworth *The Excursion*	
Stephenson invents first locomotive	**1815** Scott *Guy Mannering*	**1815** Final defeat of Napoleon at Battle of Waterloo
1815 Schubert song *The Erl-king*	Wordsworth *Collected Poems*	
	1816 Byron *Childe Harold* Canto 3, *The Prisoner of Chillon*	
	Coleridge *Christabel and Other Poems*	
	Peacock *Headlong Hall*	
	Shelley 'Hymn to Intellectual Beauty', 'Mont Blanc'	
1817 Schubert songs *The Trout* and *Death and the Maiden*	**1817** Byron *Manfred*	
Friedrich *Cemetery at Dusk* and *City at Moonrise*	Coleridge *Biographia Literaria, Sibylline Leaves*	
Hegel *Encyclopaedia of the Philosophical Sciences*	Hazlitt *Characters of Shakespeare's Plays*	
	Keats *Poems*	
	Scott *Rob Roy*	
1818 Friedrich *Wanderer above the Sea of Fog*	**1818** Austen *Northanger Abbey*	**1818** Parliament votes against universal suffrage (votes for all)
Savannah becomes the first steamship to cross the Atlantic	Byron *Childe Harold* Canto IV	
	Keats *Endymion*	
	Peacock *Nightmare Abbey*	
	Mary Shelley *Frankenstein*	
	Shelley 'Revolt of Islam', 'Ozymandias'	
1819 Schubert *Trout* Quintet	**1819** Byron *Don Juan* Cantos I, II	**1819** Working day limited to 12 hours for children in England
Géricault *The Raft of the Medusa*	Scott *Ivanhoe*	'Peterloo Massacre'
	Shelley *The Cenci*, writes 'The Mask of Anarchy' (pub. 1832)	

1820 Constable *Dedham Lock and Mill*
Henry Fuseli *Solitude at Dawn*

1821 Constable *Study of Clouds at Hampstead Heath, The Hay Wain*
Weber *Der Freischütz*
Faraday discovers basis of electromagnetic rotation

1823 Beethoven *Choral Symphony* (No.9)

1824 Delacroix *Massacre at Chios*
Friedrich *Evening, The Wreck of the Hope*
National Gallery founded in London
1825 Mendelssohn *Octet for Strings*
1826 Ampère *Electrodyamics*
1827 Schubert song-cycle *Winter Journey*
1829 Stephenson's "Rocket" runs on Liverpool to Manchester railway
1830 Berlioz *Symphonie Fantastique*
Delacroix *Liberty Leading the People*
1832 Mendelssohn *The Hebrides*

1838 Turner *The Fighting Temeraire*
1840 Schumann song cycles *A Woman's Love* and *Life, A Poet's Love*
1842 Turner *Snow storm*
1843 Verdi *The Two Foscari*
1844 Turner *Rain, Steam and Speed*

1848 Verdi *The Corsair*

1820 Blake 'Jerusalem'
Clare *Poems Descriptive of Rural Life and Scenery*
Keats *Lamia*
Shelley *Prometheus Unbound*
1821 Scott *Kenilworth*
Clare *The Village Minstrel*
Byron *Don Juan* Cantos III-V, *Marino Faliero*
De Quincey *Confessions of an English Opium Eater*
Shelley *Defence of Poetry*
1823 Lamb *Essays of Elia*
Scott *Peveril of the Peak, Quentin Durward*
Byron *Don Juan* Cantos VI–XIV
1824 Byron *Don Juan* Cantos XV-XVI
Hogg *Memoirs and Confessions of a Justified Sinner*
Scott *Redgauntlet*

1826 Scott *Woodstock*
1827 Clare *The Shepherd's Calendar with Village Stories and Other Poems*
1830 Cobbett *Rural Rides* (to 1833)
1831 Hugo *Notre Dame de Paris*
1832 Goethe *Faust* Pt 2
1834 Crabbe *Poetical Works*
1835 Wordsworth *Yarrow Revisited, and Other Poems*
1836 Coleridge *Table Talk*
1837 Carlyle *French Revolution*
1839 Shelley *Poetical Works* ed. Mary Shelley

1843 Wordsworth succeeds Southey as Poet Laureate
1847 Emily Brontë *Wuthering Heights*
Charlotte Brontë *Jane Eyre*

1850 Wordsworth's *The Prelude* published in its entirety

1820 George III dies; succeeded by George IV
Malthus *Principles of Political Economy*

1821 Start of Greek War of Independence (to 1827)

1824 Combination Act of 1799 repealed: trade unions recognized by British government

1825 First public railway opened from Stockton to Darlington

1829 Catholic Emancipation Act
1830 George IV dies; succeeded by William IV
1831 Whig government elected after many years of Tory rule
1832 Reform Act
1833 Abolition of slavery in British Empire
First Factory Act
1836 Chartists publish 'People's Charter'
1837 William IV dies; succeeded by Victoria
1842 Mines Act bans women and children from working underground
1846 Famine in Ireland
1848 Revolutions in Europe
1851 Great Exhibition displays achievements of the Industrial Revolution, science and the arts

8 5

GLOSSARY OF TERMS

absolute monarchy defines a state in which the sovereign has complete power over all matters of government.

Age of Reason (also known as the Enlightenment) a Western European literary, intellectual, philosophical and cultural climate that prevailed between roughly 1660 and 1770, and which advocated faith in clarity of thought and writing. It was thought that human reason would solve all problems, stimulating scientific discoveries and other progress.

Augustan refers in English literature to writers active during the English Augustan period (approximately the first half of the 18th century) who admired and imitated the wit, elegance and style of the Classical writers. Examples include Joseph Addison, Alexander Pope, Richard Steele and Jonathan Swift. From the stylistic point of view, some critics would include John Dryden, who wrote before 1700, and Oliver Goldsmith and Samuel Johnson, who continued writing into the later 18th century. The term originally referred to such Classical writers as Horace (65-8BC), Ovid (43BC-AD18) and Virgil (70-19BC), who were active during the reign of the Roman Emperor Augustus (27BC-AD14).

ballad a poem that tells a story, usually in the form of four-line stanzas (quatrains). Traditionally, narrative folk ballads were passed on by word of mouth from generation to generation. Examples include the legends of the rebel Robin Hood and the Border Ballads telling of skirmishes and bloodshed on the English-Scottish borders. Notable literary ballads include Keats's 'La Belle Dame sans Merci' and Oscar Wilde's 'The Ballad of Reading Gaol'.

Baroque a term used to describe a style of architecture, art and music prevalent in the 17th century. It can also be used for writing with florid and dramatic features.

Beat Movement a loose-knit group of American anti-establishment writers of the 1950s, sometimes known as the Beat Generation. Unconventional and sometimes anarchic in both writing and permissive lifestyle, they deliberately shocked middle-class Americans. They were influenced among other things by jazz and Zen Buddhism.

carpe diem (Latin: literally 'seize the day') the concept of living for the moment as opposed to spending time analyzing the past or planning for the future.

Chartism a mainly working-class radical movement of the late 1830s and 1840s whose demands for governmental reform were outlined in the 'People's Charter'. These demands included votes for all men, abolition of property qualifications and payment for MPs, voting by secret ballot, equal representation in each electoral district, and annual elections for parliament. The Chartist movement died out after the rejection of its petitions by Parliament in 1839 and 1842.

childe (as in Byron's *Childe Harold's Pilgrimage*) a title from medieval chivalric romances indicating a nobleman's eldest son who has not yet become a knight.

Doric one of the five main styles, known as 'orders', of Classical architecture.

Girondins one of the factions in the Revolutionary government of France. The name derives from the Gironde region of France, and the Girondins represented the views of the people of the provinces as opposed to those in Paris. They were opposed by the ***Jacobins***.

Gordon Riots anti-Catholic riots that took place in London in June 1870. They were named after Lord George Gordon, leader of the Protestant Association.

Gothic in architecture, a style prevalent in Western Europe from the 12th to the 15th centuries. It was characterized by pointed arches and windows, flying buttresses, and high, vaulted roofs. In literature, a style that was popular in Britain after the 1760s and which deals with the mysterious, horrific and supernatural, and which was a reaction against the *rationalism* that had gone before.

Graveyard School of Poetry refers to certain 18th-century poets who wrote reflectively about mortality and death, for example 'The Grave' by Robert Blair or Thomas Gray's 'Elegy Written in a Country Churchyard'. For a time these themes were moderately fashionable.

humanism/humanist these terms, in a literary sense, are most often used to apply to the moral and philosophical ideas (that is, 'humanities' as opposed to 'sciences') of Renaissance writers and thinkers such as Desiderius Erasmus, Sir Thomas More, Sir Philip Sidney, Edmund Spenser and, later, John Milton. Classical and Christian ideas were blended, placing at the center of thinking the achievements, dignity and positive aspects of human beings in this world, rather than their innate corruption and the spiritual afterlife. The attitude is represented in the Prince's speech 'What a piece of work is man. How noble in reason, how excellent in faculty…' in Act II, Scene 2 of Shakespeare's *Hamlet*. Later on these terms referred to the ideas of those such as Samuel Johnson and Thomas Arnold, who advocated a liberal philosophy of mankind and adopted the views of Renaissance humanists.

Ionic one of the five main styles, known as 'orders', of Classical architecture.

Jacobins One of the factions in the Revolutionary government of France, whose leaders included Maximilien Robespierre. The name comes from the location of the headquarters of the group at the premises of Jacobin (Dominican) monks in Paris. The Jacobins were opposed by the *Girondins*, but seized power during the 'Reign of Terror', 1793-4.

Luddites groups who smashed machinery on the grounds that mechanization took away their jobs. Said to be derived from Ned Ludd, who broke up some machinery in a fit of uncontrollable rage.

mechanic form a style in which a writer determines the form of a work according to a predetermined set of rules as opposed to *organic form*, in which the form is allowed to arise naturally from the subject matter and theme. The classical French dramatists of the 17th century constructed their plays according to mechanic form and looked down upon Shakespeare's preference for organic form, which they considered careless and shapeless. *Neo-Classicism* characteristically adopts mechanic forms; Romanticism takes on organic forms.

Negative Capability a phrase coined by Keats to indicate a state wherein a writer appreciates and accepts the beauty of things without endlessly striving to understand everything down to the last detail; he suppresses his own intellect and enters into an imaginative appreciation of most aspects of the surrounding world. This appreciation of imaginative response before reason is a central aspect of Romanticism.

neo-Classicism a label applied to the style of literature and other arts (such as architecture) created during the neo-Classical period. It is often contrasted with Romanticism. The neo-Classicists valued reason, intellect and a balanced outlook, distrusting the emotions. They looked back to the rational, intellectual world of Ancient Greece and Rome as models of common sense and balance. Notable neo-Classical writers include Dryden, Swift, Pope, Fielding and Goldsmith.

New Jerusalem a term used by both Blake and Wordsworth to describe their vision of an idealized city or state.

organic form a style in which the form of a work arises naturally out of the writer's subject and theme; it grows and takes shape as a living organism does and is uninhibited by a set of rules as in **mechanic form.** Shakespeare and his fellow dramatists, and Coleridge and his fellow Romantics, favored organic form.

persona (plural *personae*) originally referring to a mask worn by an actor, which was changed in order to assume a different character, the term has come to mean the identity assumed by the writer of a story or poem.

picturesque an aesthetic category that arose in the 18th century, and which lay between the 'beautiful' and the '**sublime**'. It was defined in the works of the Reverend William Gilpin and set out to view real landscapes in a painterly way. Picturesque scenes were full of variety and curious details but were neither serene (like the beautiful) nor awe-inspiring (like the sublime). Seeking out the picturesque became almost a cult in the 18th century, and many poets and other writers incorporated picturesque descriptions into their work.

pocket boroughs parliamentary seats for which there so few voters that it was in the gift (or 'pocket') of a powerful local landowner to decide who should be the Member of Parliament. For example, by the 18th century Old Sarum near Salisbury had no inhabitants, but it was owned by the Pitt family, who could vote anyone they wished as MP for that borough.

poetic diction refers to a choice of language favored by poets at any particular time. The phrase is most often applied in a condemnatory way to the idea, common among the **neo-Classical** poets of the 18th century, that poetry should be written in an artificially elevated language that should not be debased by the use of everyday words. In general, Latin-based words were preferred to Anglo-Saxon ones. Thomas Gray considered that 'the language of the age is never the language of poetry'. Examples of the poetic diction of this period are 'feathered breed' for 'birds', 'finny tribe' for 'fish', and 'milky race' for 'cows'. It was against such language that Wordsworth, Coleridge and other Romantics reacted.

post-Modernism in general, this term covers culture since 1945 (the end of the Second World War). After the confidence in progress, which is a feature of Modernism, post-Modernism reflects the kind of insecurity, doubt and sometimes nihilism caused by such events as the Nazi atrocities and the threat of extinction under the shadow of the nuclear bomb.

radical in the context of the Romantic Age, anti-establishment thinking by people who wished to change society for, as they saw it, the better. At the time, democrats were regarded as dangerous radicals, and it is easy to forget that this is how many of the Romantics poets were seen at the time; Coleridge's preaching of democracy was a treasonable offense for which a friend of his was sent to prison. Nowadays, we would describe as 'left-wing' or 'socialist' such people as Shelley, Coleridge, Wordsworth and the young Godwin.

rationalism a trend in philosophy that values reason and intellect above the emotions and imagination. It was in large part the domination of the 18th century by rationalist philosophy against which the Romantics reacted.

Rococo an architectural term referring to elegant flourishes of decorative scrollwork. It is generally applied to writing that displays flourishes of verbal dexterity and wit.

rotten boroughs a term applied to towns that retained a Member of Parliament despite having lost their traditional economic function and having few voters.

sensibility a term used to denote the ability to respond with feeling and sympathy, even empathy, to a circumstance, book or other artistic form, especially in relation to aspects of beauty or to the plight of others. The term became popular in the late 18th century.

Seven Years' War a conflict in Europe that lasted from 1756 to 1763 and involved two opposing groups of countries: Austria, France, Russia and Sweden against Prussia, Britain and Portugal. There was also fighting in North America between France and Britain; Britain eventually emerged triumphant, taking over French territories in North America.

Sturm und Drang ('Storm and Stress') a movement in German literature which foreshadowed Romanticism and rejected Classical values. The phrase comes from a play by Friedrich Klinger, a protegé of Goethe. Typical *Sturm und Drang* dramas involved belief in individual experience, rebellion and ignoring of conventions.

sublime an aesthetic category that arose in the 18th century, and which was associated with landscapes that induced feelings of awe, terror and wonder. It was a reaction to the emphasis on clarity and precision that held sway during the ***Age of Reason***. The sublime was defined in Edmund Burke's 1757 essay, entitled *A Philosophical Enquiry into the Origin of our Ideas of the Sublime and the Beautiful*.

surrealism refers to a movement in art and literature that explored 'beyond the real' in order to depict the workings of the unconscious mind.

Tory a word originally applied to Irish outlaws that was used to describe those who opposed the barring of the Roman Catholic Duke of York (later James II) from the English throne and who continued to support the Stuarts after 1689. During the 18th century the Tories grew into a political party that supported the established Church and state and opposed liberalism. During the 19th century, this movement developed into the Conservative Party.

Transcendentalism an American school of philosophy, which owed much to German Romanticism and to the English Lake District poets. The essential idea was a belief that God exists in all things in Nature. Through their intuition, Transcendentalists came to understand their connection with and place within all things in creation. The founders of the Transcendentalist movement were Henry David Thoreau and Ralph Waldo Emerson.

Unitarian defines one who believes that God is a single being, as opposed to a trinity of God the Father, God the Son, and God the Holy Ghost.

Utilitarianism a major movement in 19th-century philosophy that measured ideas and courses of action according to their apparent usefulness to mankind, and according to the number of people whose happiness was affected. The main exponents of this ethic were Jeremy Bentham and John Stuart Mill. Its critics pointed in particular to its strictly logical approach, which could seem ruthless and lacking in sympathy and sensitivity.

Whig a word of Scottish origin that applied to those who opposed James II's accession to the English throne in 1685. The Whigs became one of the two main political parties, and during the 19th century developed into the Liberal Party.

BIOGRAPHICAL GLOSSARY

Austen, Jane (1775-1817) often considered England's finest woman novelist. Born at Steventon, Hampshire, the daughter of a country parson. As a child she wrote for pleasure and later decided to concentrate on writing about the kind of local village families who lived in the world that she knew. She wrote with great wit, humor, irony and a keen interest in human nature and created a precise picture of aspects of her age with characters such as the engaging Elizabeth Bennet, the obsequious Mr Collins and the obnoxiously haughty aristocrat Lady Catherine de Burgh in *Pride and Prejudice*. Her books all deal with ideas of position, etiquette and traditions intrinsic to English society. Other notable works include *Sense and Sensibility*, *Mansfield Park*, *Emma*, *Northanger Abbey* and *Persuasion*. She lived for a time in Bath before returning to Hampshire with her mother and sister after her father's death in 1805. She died in Winchester and is buried there.

Beckford, William (1759-1844) writer. Born at Fonthill in Wiltshire, he inherited huge wealth from his father. He spent much time and money reconstructing Fonthill in the Gothic style. However, part of the building collapsed in 1825. He is mainly remembered for his Gothic novel *Vathek*.

Bentham, Jeremy (1748-1832) lawyer and writer on moral, legal and political matters. Born in London, he was educated at Westminster School and Oxford University. He studied law but never actually worked as a barrister. Some of his suggestions for legal reform have over the years been put into practice. He is best remembered for *Introduction to the Principles of Morals and Legislation* in which he set out his theory of Utilitarianism whereby moral and political acts are measured according to their usefulness. He wrote: 'It is the greatest happiness of the greatest number that is the measure of right and wrong.' In this opposition to individualism, and in his hostility to imaginative literature, he stood opposed to many of the fundamental beliefs of the Romantics.

Blake, William (1757-1827) poet and artist. Born in London and educated at home, he was apprenticed to an engraver at the age of 14. After his apprenticeship he attended the newly founded Royal Academy, although he came to disagree profoundly with the teaching there. He married Catherine Boucher in 1782. His first volume of poetry was published in 1783 (*Poetical Sketches*). His radical politics led him to befriend like-minded people such as William Godwin and Thomas Paine. He admired Milton as a great national poet but in *The Marriage of Heaven and Hell* attacked Milton's *Paradise Lost* and displayed his unorthodox aversion to Christianity and all organized religion.

He illustrated most of his writings with engravings, using a type of relief etching of his own invention. However, much of this work was not discovered until after his death. In some ways a Romantic idealist in times of industrial revolution and political unrest, his work demonstrates great depth and ranges from scathing attacks to lyrical tenderness. Notable works include *The French Revolution, Visions of the Daughters of Albion* and *Songs of Innocence and of Experience*. The Blakes lived in poverty for much of their lives, despite being taken up by a patron briefly in the early 1800s. After his death, Blake was buried in an unmarked grave in a public cemetery in London.

Burke, Edmund (1729-97) lawyer, politician, orator and man of letters. Born in Dublin, he was educated at Trinity College. He studied law but never practiced as a lawyer. Instead he moved in the London literary circle, becoming friends with Johnson, Goldsmith and many other literary figures of his day. He was first elected a Member of Parliament in 1765. A radical politician, he advocated freedom in many forms – of the House of Commons from royal control, of trade, of the Irish, of slaves, and of the American colonies. He was admired in later life by Wordsworth, who paid tribute to him in *The Prelude*. Notable works include *A Philosophical Enquiry into the Origin of Our Ideas of the Sublime and the Beautiful* and *Reflections on the Revolution in France*.

Burns, Robert (1759-96) poet. Born in Alloway, Ayrshire, the son of a tenant farmer. Even after he became famous he retained a sense of his humble rural background, which is reflected in his work. After the success of his first volume of poetry, *Poems Chiefly in the Scottish Dialect*, he moved to Edinburgh where he was sometimes patronized as a 'ploughman poet' – a kind of rustic genius. He returned to farming in 1788 but suffered in a time of agricultural economic hardship; he was forced to abandon the farm in 1791 and ended his days in Dumfries. He was able to write in the formal English of the day and in vernacular Scots, sometimes combining the two. He was also an avid collector, writer and re-writer of traditional Scottish songs, most famously *Auld Lang Syne* and *Red, Red Rose*. He achieved a cult status during his lifetime and today is widely regarded as the national poet of Scotland. Notable works include 'The Cotter's Saturday Night' and 'Halloween' (both in *Poems Chiefly in the Scottish Dialect)*, *Holy Willie's Prayer* and *Tam O'Shanter*.

Byron, George Gordon, Lord (1788-1824) poet and playwright. Born in London, he was the son of Catherine Gordon, a Scottish heiress, and Captain 'Mad Jack' Byron who squandered his wife's money and fled to France to escape his creditors not long after his son's birth. In 1798, the death of a great-uncle meant that Byron inherited Newstead Abbey in Nottinghamshire and a baronetcy, although very little money came with the house or title. He was educated at Harrow School and Cambridge University, where he gained a reputation for his high-spirited behavior. He affected to despise 'scribbling', as he called writing, and asked, "Who would write who had anything better to do?" But in 1812 he published the first part of *Childe Harold's Pilgrimage*, after which he said, "I awoke one morning and found myself famous." Among other qualities, his poetry expresses by turns lyrical beauty and biting satire, and its intense popularity, especially among a female readership, became known as 'Byronmania'. Celebrated for his lifestyle as much as his writing, he doubtless played up to Lady Caroline Lamb's image of him as 'mad, bad, and dangerous to know'. He married Annabella Millbanke in 1815, and they had a daughter in the same year. But the marriage was not a success; Annabella left Byron, and in the face of huge public disapproval Byron left Britain in 1816, never to return. He stayed with the Shelleys in Switzerland before travelling on to Italy, and his fame soon spread across Europe. In 1823 he sailed for Greece to help the Greeks in their fight for independence from the Turks. He died of rheumatic fever in the following year. Notable works include *The Giaour*, *The Bride of Abydos*, *The Corsair*, *Lara*, 'The Prisoner of Chillon', *Manfred* and *Don Juan*.

Chatterton, Thomas (1752-70) see main text on page 13.

Clare, John (1793-1864) poet. Usually categorized as a rural poet, he was much attached to his native village of Helpston, Northamptonshire, where he was an agricultural laborer. He wrote with clarity and truth about the countryside that he knew so well. His poetry was at first fashionable, but a decline in the popularity of 'ploughman poets' contributed to his growing insanity, and he spent the last years of his life in Northampton General Asylum. Thanks to the attention of various 20th-century poets, his work has once again become known and admired. Notable works include *The Village Minstrel* and *The Shepherd's Calendar*.

Coleridge, Samuel Taylor (1772-1834) poet, critic and translator. He was the youngest son of the vicar of Ottery St Mary, Devon. He was educated at Christ's Hospital, London, and Cambridge University. In 1793 he joined the Light Dragoons under the alias Silas Tomkyn Comberbache but was dismissed under an insanity clause. He met Robert Southey in the following year and became involved in a plot to set up an idealistic commune in North America. Known as the 'Pantisocracy' scheme, it eventually came to nothing. However, the scheme required Coleridge to have a wife, and as a result he entered into an ultimately unhappy marriage with Sara Fricker, Southey's sister-in-law. The pair had a son, Hartley, in 1796. At about this time, Coleridge met Wordsworth, and their relationship, especially the collaboration over the *Lyrical Ballads*, affected the direction of English poetry and was a keystone in English Romanticism. In 1799 Coleridge met and fell in love with Sara Hutchinson, Wordsworth's future sister-in-law, and at the same time his own marriage began to fail. He was formally separated from his wife in 1806. Addicted to opium, he fell out with Wordsworth and went through a period of despair, but recovered from his addiction at a house in Highgate, London, where he lived from 1816 until his death. Inventive, imaginative and exciting, Coleridge's small but brilliant poetic output is characterized by a sense of insecurity. He was an influential critic and thinker, and his theories on such matters as the poetic imagination, organic form and the Elizabethan stage contributed much to literary criticism in general and to our understanding of Romanticism in particular. Notable works include 'Kubla Khan', 'The Rime of the Ancient Mariner' (published in *Lyrical Ballads*), 'Frost at Midnight', 'Dejection: An Ode', and *Biographia Literaria*.

Crabbe, George (1755-1832) poet. He was born in Aldeburgh, Suffolk, trained as a surgeon and set up a practice in Aldeburgh. In 1780, he decided to follow a literary career and went to London, where he was helped by Edmund Burke. He became a priest and was vicar of parishes in Leicestershire and Wiltshire. Much of his early poetry is Augustan in the manner of Pope; his later narrative verse is more akin to the Romantics. Inspired by the landscape of his native Suffolk, he created a picture of an often poor and degraded rural life. Among his friends or admirers he counted Austen, Byron, Johnson, Scott, Southey and Wordsworth. Notable works include *The Village* and *The Borough* (including 'Peter Grimes').

De Quincey, Thomas (1785-1859) literary critic and journalist. Born in Manchester, he read *Lyrical Ballads* in 1800 and became determined to meet Wordsworth, although diffidence and feelings of inadequacy meant that the encounter would not take place for another seven years. He began to take opium in 1804 and gradually became an addict, which eventually led to his estrangement from the Wordsworths. After spending a modest inheritance, he turned to writing as a way to support himself and his family. His writing on aspects of the way the mind works had considerable influence on Poe, among others. Notable works include *Confessions of an English Opium Eater*.

Godwin, William (1756-1836) see box on page 16.

Hazlitt, William (1778-1830) essayist, literary critic and theatre critic. He was born in Maidstone, Kent. His father was a Unitarian minister, and William also trained for the ministry before becoming disillusioned with religion. He was a lifelong radical who supported the French Revolution and was deeply concerned about social conditions in Britain. His prose was highly esteemed, especially his writings on contemporary authors, politics and Elizabethan playwrights. He was also a fine critic of the early Romantics. Notable works include *Characters of Shakespeare's Plays*, *Lectures on English Poets*, *English Comic Writers*, *My First Acquaintance with Poets*, *The Spirit of the Age* and *The Plain Speaker*.

Keats, John (1795-1821) poet. Son of a London stable manager and innkeeper, in 1811 he began training as an apothecary-surgeon, qualifying at Guy's Hospital in 1816 as a Licentiate of the Society of Apothecaries. He soon abandoned medicine to write poetry. Through the editor of the journal *The Examiner*, James Leigh Hunt, he met Hazlitt, Lamb and Shelley. He became a leading figure in Romanticism, highly regarded by contemporaries such as Shelley, although attacked by right-wing reviewers as a 'Cockney poet'. He was a very versatile poet; his work includes sonnets, odes, narrative poems, children's poetry and other forms. His writing is noted for wit, sensitivity, use of the senses, medievalism, creation of interior landscapes and escapism. He was not so directly political or social in his comments as some of his contemporaries, such as Blake, Shelley and Byron. He thought deeply about literary concepts, including his notion of Negative Capability (see Glossary of Terms). In 1818 he met Fanny Brawne, with whom he fell deeply but unhappily in love, and in 1829 he contracted tuberculosis. He went to Italy, accompanied by his friend the painter Joseph Severn, to try to recover his health. His early death in Rome has tended to add to his Romantic mystique. Notable works include *Endymion*, 'To Autumn', 'The Eve of St Agnes', 'La Belle Dame sans Merci', 'Isabella', 'Ode to a Nightingale' and 'Ode on a Grecian Urn'.

Lamb, Charles (1775-1834) essayist, poet, letter writer, children's book writer and literary critic. Born in London, he went to Christ's Hospital with Coleridge, of whom he was a lifelong friend. He worked at East India House until his retirement. In addition to Coleridge, he was close to Southey, Leigh Hunt and Wordsworth and had an influence upon all of them. His preference for reading Shakespeare might be attributed to the low state of theatre during his life. Notable works include *Tales From Shakespear* [sic], which he wrote in collaboration with his sister, Mary (1764-1847) and *Specimens of the English Dramatic Poets who Lived about the Time of Shakespeare*.

Paine, Thomas (1737-1809) see box on page 22.

Peacock, Thomas Love (1785-1866) satirist, poet and essayist. Born in Weymouth, he lived on his inheritance until he was in his thirties, when he took a post at East India House. He was a lifelong friend of Shelley, to whom he became a kind of literary adviser. Amusing, clever and radical, some of his stories and settings are parodies of the kind of Gothic romance that was popular at the time. Notable works include *Headlong Hall*, *Nightmare Abbey*, *Maid Marian*, *Crotchet Castle* and *Gryll Grange*.

Radcliffe, Ann (1764-1823) novelist. Born in London, she married William Radcliffe in 1786. He was later editor of *The English Chronicle*. She became well-known for her Gothic novels, including *The Mysteries of Udolpho* and *The Italian*.

Scott, Sir Walter (1771-1832) novelist, poet, critic and editor. Born in Edinburgh, he was educated at Edinburgh High School and Edinburgh University. He studied law and entered the Scottish Bar but gave up the law to concentrate on writing and editorial work. His early writing was nearly all poetry, including verse romances on historical or legendary subjects such as 'The Lay of the Last Minstrel'. However, partly prompted by the success of Byron's *Childe Harold's Pilgrimage*, which he regarded as superior to anything he could achieve in poetry, he turned to historical romances in novel form. The great popularity of *Waverley* confirmed the decision, giving Scott immediate success and international fame and turning him into the most widely read novelist of his time. His descriptions of ruins and landscapes helped to define Romanticism, and his settings stimulated interest in medievalism and the historical novel. Scott, a patriot and a Unionist, was the first writer to be knighted. Other notable works include *Guy Mannering*, *Rob Roy*, *The Heart of Midlothian*, *The Bride of Lammermoor*, *Ivanhoe*, *Peveril of the Peak* and *Redgauntlet*.

Shelley, Mary (1797-1851) novelist, biographer and editor. She was the only daughter of William Godwin and Mary Wollstonecraft, who died a few days after giving birth to her. She ran away with Shelley at the age of 16, marrying him in 1816 after the death of his first wife. Time spent in Switzerland and Italy with her husband and Byron influenced her choice of settings, especially in her best-known work, the Gothic novel *Frankenstein, or The Modern Prometheus*. She often used the types of historical themes that were characteristic of Romanticism. Other notable works include *The Last Man*.

Shelley, Percy Bysshe (1792-1822) poet, translator and playwright. Son of a Member of Parliament and heir to a minor baronetcy, he rebelled against authority all his life. Educated at Eton College and Oxford University, he was expelled from University College for writing a pamphlet entitled *The Necessity of Atheism*. In 1811 he eloped with the 16-year-old Harriet Westbrook, but the marriage failed in 1813. The following year, Shelley met and fell in love with Mary Shelley, and, abandoning Harriet and their two children, he ran away with Mary. Harriet drowned herself in 1816, and Shelley married Mary soon after. In 1818 he left England for good and settled in Italy. He was drowned off the coast of Italy during a storm. His highly imaginative writing was much inspired by political views: he exemplifies the radical intellectual aspects of Romanticism and opposed tyranny, oppression and injustice. 'Freedom!' and 'Liberty!' were his war cries, and his technically masterful poetry is exuberant, humorous and visionary. Notable works include 'Queen Mab', 'Ozymandius', 'The Mask of Anarchy', 'Ode to the West Wind', *The Cenci*, *The Defence of Poetry*, 'To a Skylark', 'The Cloud', *Prometheus Unbound*, 'Adonais' and 'When the Lamp is Shattered'.

Southey, Robert (1774-1843) poet, historian, essayist, biographer and prolific man of letters. He was educated at Westminster School and Oxford University. He became a friend of Coleridge and planned a 'Pantisocratic' community in America. The plans, however, came to nothing. He secretly married Edith Fricker in 1795 and persuaded Coleridge into an unhappy marriage with her sister, Sara. He bought Greta Hall in Keswick and was on the fringe of the Lake poets. Like Wordsworth, he changed politically from a radical to a Tory as he grew older, and this did not endear him to the second phase of Romantics. He became Poet Laureate in 1813. Notable works include *Palmerin of England* and *A Vision of Judgement*.

Walpole, Horace (1717-97) letter writer, novelist, editor and verse dramatist. Born in London, he was the youngest son of Sir Robert Walpole. He was educated at Eton College and Cambridge University. In 1741 he moved into Strawberry Hill in Twickenham and embarked on a project to redesign it in the Gothic style. This remodelling was to continue for 25 years. He also wrote the first Gothic novel *The Castle of Otranto*. In 1769, Chatterton (see page 13) sent some of his forged verses to Walpole, but despite showing some initial interest, Walpole soon found out the truth about Chatterton's work. Walpole's many letters were written with an eye to publication – he requested the return of many of them, which he annotated for future editors. More than 4000 of them appear in a 48-volume edition.

Wollestonecraft, Mary (1759-97) social and political writer, novelist and translator. Born in London, she was largely self-taught. She set up a school, which was unsuccessful, but which prompted her to write *Thoughts on the Education of Daughters*. After a time as a governess, she decided to make her living by writing and took work as a translator and reviewer. Sometimes called the founder of modern feminism, she also wrote *A Vindication of the Rights of Woman*. After a failed love affair, she met and married William Godwin, the radical thinker and writer. She died after giving birth to their daughter, the future Mary Shelley.

Wordsworth, Dorothy (1771-1855) journal writer. She was a major literary influence upon her brother William. She did not write for publication, but Wordsworth drew extensively from her journals as a literary source. Notable works include her *Grasmere Journal*, which covers the period 1800-03, from which William drew for his famous poem 'I Wandered Lonely as a Cloud'. She went with her brother to Germany in 1798-9 and accompanied him on numerous walking tours. She lived with William and, after 1802, with his wife and family for most of her life.

Wordsworth, William (1770-1850) poet. Born in Cockermouth, Westmorland, the son of a steward on the Lonsdale estate. Both his parents died while he was young. He attended Hawkshead Grammar School and Cambridge University. In 1790 he walked 2000 miles through France and the Alps during his university vacation. In 1791 he returned to France, and in 1792 he fell in love with Annette Vallon, with whom he had a daughter. His work was first published in 1793 – 'An Evening Walk' and *Descriptive Sketches*. A key figure in English Romanticism, the political radicalism of his youth and the conservatism of his age is somewhat reflected in his writings. He was much influenced by his association with Coleridge in Somerset in the 1790s and later in the Lake District, and by the lifelong support of his beloved sister, Dorothy. In 1802 he married Mary Hutchison and enjoyed a happy marriage that produced many children. He did much to change the course of English poetry in two crucial ways: he rejected neo-Classical poetic diction and aimed to write in 'the ordinary language of ordinary men', and he wrote about everyday things and people. He is closely associated with the topography and people of his native Lake District where he spent much of his life. His best work was written before 1810, after which he revised much of his early poetry, often to its disadvantage. Notable works include *Lyrical Ballads* (with Coleridge), 'Resolution and Independence', 'Intimations of Immortality from Recollections of Early Childhood', *The Excursion* and *The Prelude*.

FURTHER READING

Chapters 1 and 2 Romanticism and **The Age of Revolution**

Ackroyd, Peter. *Chatterton*. 1986. Reprint, New York: Grove/Atlantic, Inc., 1996.

Berlin, Isaiah. *The Roots of Romanticism*. Princeton, NJ: Princeton University Press, 1999.

Godwin, William. *Enquiry Concerning Political Justice and Its Influence on Morals and Happiness*. Edited by F. E. L. Priestley. 1946. Reprint, Toronto, Canada: University of Toronto Press, 1969.

Gurr, Elizabeth. *English Literature in Context*. Oxford, England: Oxford University Press, 2000.

Heath, Duncan and Judy Boreham. *Introducing Romanticism*. New York: Totem Books, 2000.

Paine, Thomas. *The Rights of Man*. 1791. Reprint, edited by Eric Foner. New York: Penguin, 1984.

Pirie, David B., ed. *Penguin History of Literature, Vol. 5: The Romantic Period*. New York: Penguin, 1994.

Shelley, Percy Bysshe. *A Defence of Poetry*. 1820. Reprint, edited by John E. Jordan. Indianapolis, IN: Bobbs-Merrill, 1965. Contains Shelley's thoughts on poetry in general and his contemporaries in particular.

Watson, J. R. *English Poetry of the Romantic Period, 1789–1830*. London: Longman, 1992.

Chapter 3 Individualism

Alexander, Meena. *Women in Romanticism*. Lanham, MD: Rowman & Littlefield, Inc., 1989.

Barzun, Jacques. *Classic, Romantic, and Modern*. 1975. Reprint, Chicago: University of Chicago Press, 1990.

Chapter 4 Economic and Social Contexts

Ackroyd, Peter. *Blake: A Biography*. New York: Alfred A. Knopf, 1996.

Mellor, Anne K., ed. *Romanticism and Feminism*. Bloomington: Indiana University Press, 1988.

Thompson, E. P. *The Making of the English Working Class*. 1963. Reprint, New York: Random House, 1985.

Chapter 5 Painting, Music, and Theatre

Einstein, Alfred. *Music in the Romantic Era*. 1947. Reprint, New York: W. W. Norton, 1975.

Gombrich, E.H. *The Story of Art*. 1950. Reprint, Upper Saddle River, NJ: Prentice Hall, 1995. See Chapter 24, 'The Break in Tradition'.

Lamb, Charles. *Elia and the Last Essays of Elia*. Edited by Jonathan Bate. Oxford, England: Oxford University Press, 1988.

Vaughan, William. *Romanticism and Art*. New York: W. W. Norton, 1996.

Chapter 6 The Gothic and Supernatural

Clark, Kenneth. *The Gothic Revival*. 1964. Reprint, London: John Murray Publishers, 1996. A discussion of Gothic Romantic architecture, including Walpole's Strawberry Hill.

Praz, Mario. *The Romantic Agony*. 1960. Reprint, translated by Angus Davidson. Oxford, England: Oxford University Press, 1990. The Gothic placed in a European context.

Tompkins, J. M. S. *The Popular Novel in England, 1770–1800*. 1932. Reprint, Westport, CT: Greenwood Publishing Group, 1976. The Gothic novel placed in its literary context.

General

Butler, Marilyn. *Romantics, Rebels and Reactionaries: English Literature and its Background, 1760–1830*. New York: Oxford University Press, 1985.

Gaull, Marion. *English Romanticism: The Human Context*. New York: W. W. Norton.

Honour, Hugh. *Romanticism*. New York: Harper and Row, 1979.

Schama, Simon. *Landscape and Memory*. New York: Alfred A. Knopf, 1995.

Simpson, David. *Romanticism, Nationalism, and the Revolt Against Theory*. Chicago: University of Chicago Press, 1993.

Thompson, E. P. *Witness Against the Beast: William Blake and the Moral Law*. Cambridge, England: Cambridge University Press, 1993.

Williams, Raymond. *Culture and Society 1780–1950*. New York: Columbia University Press, 1994.

Wu, Duncan, ed. *Romanticism: An Anthology*, 2nd edition. Oxford, England: Blackwell Publishers, 2000. A fairly comprehensive anthology including a CD-ROM with much useful background material.

Websites

http://www.artcyclopedia.com/ The site gives a good overview of Romantic painting.

http://www.hearts-ease.org/library/romantic Useful information, including 55 pages on context.

http://www.library.utoronto.ca/utel/rp/authors/ Gives details of all the major writers and displays many of their major poems.

http://www.romantic-poetry.com Essays on poetry of the Romantic era.

http://iris.nyit.edu/~dhogsett/romanticsunbound/ Various aspects of the Romantics are covered, including art, music, and the Gothic.

http://www.library.utoronto.ca/utel/rp/poems/ A useful website on which all indexes can be searched for poets, first lines, whole texts, criticism, topics, and dates of publication.

http://www.unm.edu/~garyh/romantic/romantic. htm A general website on many aspects of English and American Romanticism.

http://www.wordsworthlakes.co.uk/default.htm For the contexts of Wordsworth homes at Cockermouth, Grasmere, and Rydal.

INDEX

INDEX